ELIZABETH BOWEN

By

Allan E. Austin

Elizabeth Bowen is the first full-length consideration of this distinguished twentieth-century Anglo-Irish writer based on her ten novels and a substantial selection of her short stories. In addition to being highly descriptive, the study indicates the relationships which exist among her fictions, and outlines the development of her thematic concerns. The author distinguishes the relative merits of her works, and establishes a context which discloses the full significance of *The Death of the Heart,* a book Walter Allen terms "one of the best English novels of the century." Perhaps the most provocative criticism occurs in the chapter which suggests that Miss Bowen writes three distinct types of short stories. The book concludes with a brief survey of Bowen criticism and includes an annotated bibliography.

ABOUT THE AUTHOR

Allan E. Austin is an Associate Professor of English at the University of Guelph, Guelph, Ontario. A journalist and freelance writer in Canada for several years before beginning his academic career, he has taught at the University of Rochester and Russell Sage College. His particular area of interest is twentieth-century British fiction and his previous critical work has been on the shorter fiction of D. H. Lawrence.

Twayne's English Authors Series

Sylvia E. Bowman, *Editor*

INDIANA UNIVERSITY

Elizabeth Bowen

t: Angus McBean

ELIZABETH BOWEN

ELIZABETH BOWEN

By ALLAN E. AUSTIN
University of Guelph

Twayne Publishers, Inc.   ::   New York

For My Family

Preface

Elizabeth Bowen's considerable critical reputation rests largely on her skill as a stylist, but the challenge posed by her art makes her essentially a coterie novelist. This former fact is regrettable because the focus upon Miss Bowen as stylist has detracted from her as a commentator on life in the modern world. She is, in fact, a wise and relevant voice, but until this view gains credence her acceptance by a larger audience remains doubtful.

This study is intended as a general introduction to Miss Bowen's fiction. I have written basically for readers who have read one or two of her novels and who, initially, may wish to compare their reading of this allusive author with commentaries grounded in the over-all fictional world; this intent need not, however, preclude the book's usefulness to those more conversant with the Bowen canon. I hope it is not critically heretical to admit I am less concerned with encouraging readers to read beyond *The Death of the Heart* and *The Heat of the Day*, her best novels (although some of her fine short stories are equally fine), than I am with placing these books in a perspective for rereading with new awareness and reward.

I recently read a review of a monograph on a British novelist in which the reviewer deprecated the adulatory treatment such books afford their subject to the detriment of any discriminating judgments. I grant that this writer identifies a very real abuse, but I hope such books are written out of enthusiasm for at least the peak of an author's work lest we have studies without any soul. I have sought to strike a balance. I confess at once a partiality to Miss Bowen's best; I believe I do her no disservice in pointing out the limitations of her remaining work.

In Chapter 1, a biographical sketch precedes a discussion of both Miss Bowen's major thematic concerns and her style. The next three chapters treat the ten novels. Chapter 5 investigates a representative selection of short stories. The final chapter briefly surveys the major criticism about Miss Bowen's works.

For permission to quote from material in copyright, I am grateful to Elizabeth Bowen and to the following publishers: to Alfred A. Knopf, Inc., the American publishers of *Joining Charles* (1929); *To the North* (1932); *The Cat Jumps* (1934); *The House in Paris* (1935); *The Death of the Heart* (1938); *Look at All Those Roses* (1941); *Bowen's Court* (1942); *Ivy Gripped the Steps* (1946); *The Heat of the Day* (1948); *Collected Impressions* (1950); *Early Stories* (1950); *The Last September* (1952); *A World of Love* (1955); *Stories by Elizabeth Bowen* (1959); *The Little Girls* (1964); *Eva Trout* (1969); to The Dial Press, the American publishers of *The Hotel* (1927); *Friends and Relations* (1931); and to Professor C. M. Bowra, Weidenfeld and Nicholson, his British publishers, and Harvard University Press, the American publishers of his *Memories 1898-1939*.

I wish to express my appreciation for thoughtful assistance to Miss Sylvia Bowman, and to three of my colleagues, Nancy Bailey, Morris Wolfe, and, especially, Doug Riggs.

ALLAN E. AUSTIN

University of Guelph

Contents

Chronology

1899   Elizabeth Bowen born in Dublin.
1916   Completes formal education at Downe House School.
1923   *Encounters*. Married to Alan Charles Cameron.
1927   *The Hotel*.
1928   Inherited Bowen's Court, County Cork.
1929   *Joining Charles; The Last September*.
1931   *Friends and Relations*.
1932   *To the North*.
1934   *The Cat Jumps*.
1935   *The House in Paris*.
1938   *The Death of the Heart*.
1941   *Look at All Those Roses*.
1942   *Bowen's Court*.
1945   *The Demon Lover;* published in the United States as *Ivy Gripped the Steps*.
1948   Miss Bowen made a Commander of the British Empire in the birthday honors.
1949   *The Heat of the Day*. Received honorary Doctor of Letters degree, Trinity College, Dublin.
1950   *Collected Impressions*.
1952   Husband died.
1955   *A World of Love*.
1957   Received honorary Doctor of Letters degree, Oxford University.
1962   *Afterthoughts*.
1964   *The Little Girls*.
1965   *A Day in the Dark*.
1969   *Eva Trout*.

Elizabeth Bowen

CHAPTER 1

The Bowen World

> "She had no source of knowledge he hadn't equally—except of course that she might have finer nerves. That was what women had where they were interested; they made out things, where people were concerned, that the people often couldn't have made out for themselves. Their nerves, their sensibility, their imagination, were conductors and revealers. . . ."
>
> —Henry James, "The Beast in the Jungle"

I *Biography*

When Elizabeth Bowen published her first book of fiction, *Encounters*, a collection of short stories, in 1923, she was twenty-four, newly married to Alan Charles Cameron, and living in Old Headington outside Oxford, in whose school system her husband was employed. The Camerons spent twelve years here; and Miss Bowen, in the first flush of her writing career, enjoyed one of her most fruitful periods. Her first four novels in addition to two further collections of short stories were written in Old Headington. Socially, the Camerons moved in the intellectual circles of Oxford University; one of their friends, the distinguished Classics scholar C. M. Bowra has provided us with a very fine characterization of Miss Bowen which reads, in part:

She was tall and very well built and had the manners of someone who has lived in the country and knows its habits. She was handsome in an unusual way, with a face that indicated both mind and character. Unlike some Irish, she did not talk for effect but kept the conversation at a high level and gave

her full attention to it. She had a slight stutter which added force to her
remarks. She had the fine style of a great lady, who on rare occasions was
not shy of slapping down impertinence, but she came from a society where
the decorum of the nineteenth century had been tempered by an Irish
frankness. With all her sensibility and imagination, she had a masculine
intelligence which was fully at home in large subjects and general ideas,
and when she sometimes gave a lecture, it was delivered with a force and
control of which most University teachers would be envious. Though she
was entirely at home in the modern world and deeply committed to it, she
had her roots in a more spacious and more assured society.[1]

This portrait of an elegant and intelligent woman bears a remark-
able affinity in style to the fiction Miss Bowen herself creates.

In 1928, when Miss Bowen's father, Henry Bowen, died, she
inherited the family estate, Bowen's Court, near Kildorrery, County
Cork; she was the first woman ever to do so since the completion of
the home in 1776. She occupied Bowen's Court following the death
of her husband in 1952 and resided there until 1960, after which
she sold it and returned to Old Headington. [2] Of Welsh extraction,
the Bowens acquired Irish lands in the seventeenth century as a
reward for services rendered Oliver Cromwell.

Although Miss Bowen was born in Dublin on June 7, 1899, her
upbringing was largely English. When she was seven she and her
mother, Florence Colley Bowen, left Dublin for Kent after her
barrister father began a protracted recovery from "brain fever."
Her mother died in Hythe in 1912. Miss Bowen received her education at the Downe House School, Westérham, Kent; after completing her schooling there in 1916, she returned to Dublin for the
duration of World War I to work in a hospital for shell-shocked
veterans. In 1918, Miss Bowen arrived in London to study at the
London Council School of Art, but she soon withdrew to travel on
the Continent.

After 1935, when the Camerons moved to Regent's Park, London,
she began to publish a book of fiction almost every other year and
also to write reviews and articles for *The New Statesman* and other
publications. She was active in London literary circles and became
acquainted with members of the Bloomsbury group, especially
with Virginia Woolf. The fiction of the latter can only have confirmed Miss Bowen in her particular manner of viewing the world.
She shares with Mrs. Woolf a sensitive airiness of comprehension,
though she records a solider reality.

The Camerons remained in London during World War II, and Miss Bowen wrote for the Ministry of Information and worked as an air-raid warden. Almost always a writer about the current scene in her fiction, Miss Bowen was never more topical than in her war-time collection of stories, *The Demon Lover* (1945), and in her wartime novel, *The Heat of the Day* (1949). During the 1940's, she was the regular book reviewer for *The Tatler*, and in the late 1950's she was an associate editor of *London Magazine*. Mr. Cameron, who had never been well as a consequence of World War I wounds, died in 1952.

Broad recognition came to Miss Bowen in the postwar years. In 1948 she was made a Commander of the British Empire (C.B.E.). In 1949, Trinity College, Dublin, honored her with an honorary Doctor of Letters degree; Oxford University awarded her the same degree eight years later.

Miss Bowen published her most recent novel, *Eva Trout*, in 1968. Throughout her writing career in addition to fiction, she has written several other books, of travel, history, criticism, and personal reminiscence. Undeniably, she has been a lady of letters in the fullest sense.

II *Context and Vision*

There is only a single allusion to T. S. Eliot's work, to *The Waste Land*, in all of Elizabeth Bown's fiction. Since T. S. Eliot is largely responsible for the predominate image in English of the modern world as fragmented and sterile, we may properly say that her fiction begins where such a poem as "The Love Song of J. Alfred Prufrock" leaves off. It is as though Miss Bowen, having seen Prufrock withdraw from society, has asked herself how vital human feelings and meaningful human relationships might be reclaimed from the paralysis gripping so many sensitive modern men and women. Miss Bowen has never doubted the validity of Eliot's early diagnosis, but she has refused to accept it as the final word on life. She has written, "Our century, as it takes its frantic course, seems barely habitable by humans: we have to learn to survive while we learn to write" (or, for most of us, to live).[3] It is the course followed, for the most part unconsciously, by her protagonists: they seek to keep themselves intact, to engage life, and to live passably until they learn to live meaningfully.

What makes Elizabeth Bowen a relevant and valuable novelist

initially is her stolid capacity to confront the chaos of the twentieth century without blenching and to counter it with a sturdy British determination to carry on. Her concept of existence, as expressed in *Collected Impressions* (1950), is grounded upon a view of life as struggle, or struggle as life: "this struggle for life, a struggle that goes on everywhere, that may be said, in fact, to be life itself . . . should not therefore have anything terrible about it. . ." (197). To Miss Bowen, the greatest single fact about our century has been its terrifying propensity for change. As true children of their times, Miss Bowen's characters confront dislocation and mutability, not as enduring truths borne out by aging and death, but as everyday conditions of life.

But Miss Bowen chooses not to view even radical alteration as necessarily evil, though she assumes at times the typically modern stance of ambivalence when she deals with the theme of change. In *The Last September* (1929), for example, when a great Irish house rich in tradition perishes in "the troubles," she views the loss as both regrettable and purgative. More typically, she is prepared to proceed on the assumption that our attitude to change, rather than the physical fact itself, determines the likely success of living with it, as exemplified by this key passage from *To the North* (1932), which, interestingly enough, begins with the image of a destroyed house:

When a great house has been destroyed by fire—left with walls bleached and ghastly and windows gaping with the cold sky—the master has not, perhaps, the heart or the money to rebuild. Trees that were its companions are cut down and the estate sold up to the speculator. Villas spring up in red rows, each a home for someone, enticing brave shops, radiant picture palaces: perhaps a park is left round the lake, where couples go boating. Lovers' lanes in aspahlt replace the lonely green rides; the obelisk having no approaches is taken away. After dark—where once there was silence a tree's shadow drawn slowly across the grass by the moon, or no moon, an exhalation of darkness—rows of windows come out like lanterns in pink and orange; boxed in bright light hundreds of lives repeat their pattern; wireless picks up a tune from street to street. Shops stream light on the pavements, upon the commotion of late shopping: big buses swarm to the kerb, small cars dart home to the garage, bicycling children flit through the birdless dark. Bright facades of cinemas reflect on to ingoing faces the expectation of pleasure: lovers laugh, gates click, doors swing, lights go on upstairs, couples lie down on honest beds. Life here is liveable, kindly and sometimes gay; there is not a ghost of space or silence; the great house with its radiation of avenues is forgotten. When spring is sweet in the air, snowdrops under the paling, when blue autumn blurs the trim streets' perspective or the low sun in winter dazzles the windows' gold—something touches the heart, disturbed, pauses, hand on a villa gate. But not to ask: What was here? (136-37)

This material would have lent itself very readily to a depiction of the wasteland, but its significance is that Miss Bowen chooses to move in the opposite direction. What inkling of nostalgic loss shows through is more than offset by the prevailing sense of opportunity and excitement.

General mutability need not inhibit life, but it undeniably makes the achievement of healthy outlooks more difficult—and it also makes routine day to day living more trying. The loss of prescribed modes of conduct and of stable moral standards has disclosed modern characters to possess what their novelistic predecessors seemingly lacked—nervous systems. As Miss Bowen states in *Collected Impressions* (1950), she believes that

the decline of manners in the grand and fixed sense has made behaviour infinitely more difficult. A perpetual, forced recourse to instinct . . . gives our friends a harassed, unstable air. There is no longer the safety of the prescribed world, of which the thousand-and-one rules could be learnt, in which one could steer one's way instructed and safe. The world, even the great world, can have, in an age of manners, held no more terrors than does the Hyde Park Corner traffic, with its apparent complexity, for the assuming driver who has passed the test. (67)

The broad lines of Miss Bowen's work appear when we see that she places essentially uneasy and nervous characters in a context which exudes the tentative and that she calmly surveys the whole through her poised narrative mask.

Some critics have related Miss Bowen's work to the most traditional of British novel forms, the comedy of manners, because she undoubtedly deals with a largely feminine cast engaged in womanly matters, with circumstances where social niceties are relevant, and where love and marriage are foremost concerns. But this association does not exhaust the nature of her work. Coming in the wake of the great experimental masters, Miss Bowen astutely applied their new esthetic self-consciousness to more typical or normative modes of behavior to produce what may be termed the modern comedy of manners. James Hill rightly sees Elizabeth Bowen as "a born consolidator" as well as "one of the few radical explorers in the recent novel."[4] Her place in the history of the British novel is assured by her ability to achieve a compromise of a high order between older modes, newer techniques, and contemporary atmospheres.

Miss Bowen has been linked at one time or another with Jane Austen, George Eliot, Virginia Woolf, and E. M. Forster; and appropriately enough, since Miss Bowen partakes of Miss Austen's tasteful wit, with Miss Eliot's moral ethic of perception, Miss Woolf's poetic style, and Forster's regard for vitalism. Perhaps Walter Allen has been as pertinent as anyone in seeing her work as "Henry James . . . superimposed upon Jane Austen," [5] in its suggested association of the subjective and objective, of the claustraphobic and open. But to any list of progenitors should be added D. H. Lawrence, for Miss Bowen's central concern with human feelings must inevitably link her to "the foremost emotional realist of the century."[6] Like Lawrence, Miss Bowen sees the essential being residing in the state of feelings; moreover, the quality of an individual's life is directly related to the depth and honesty of his felt life. Perhaps in an age in which the human mind has shown its limitations in the face of perpetual flux and overwhelming data, the possibilities for survival, as propounded by Lawrence and by Miss Bowen, truly reside in the emotional being. This fresh regard for emotional health undoubtedly has contributed to the current vogue Lawrence is enjoying. In her own way, whether deliberately or not, Miss Bowen has domesticated much of Lawrence.

Human beings, as Miss Bowen sees them in *The Death of the Heart* (1938), are born with an extensive capacity for self-assertion and with a relentless desire for self-realization; in the words of one of her characters, "We are minor in everything but our passions" (46). These passions she calls "a sort of lunatic giant," indicating both their strength and irresponsibility. Lunatic giants are likely to be untrustworthy and dangerous fellows, and so they often prove to be in her stories. They are also real; and, though they are "impossible socially," they must be given elbow room.[7] Inevitably, an individual's feelings are blunted against society's corporate ego, and then the giant's tenderness, his almost neurotic fear of hurt, is revealed. Damaged feelings are a fate all sensitive beings are destined to experience; they are Miss Bowen's version of the fall from innocence. No individual who has not been bruised can be saved, but not all who are bruised are saved.

Some critics, confronting Miss Bowen's early work, in which she was heuristically finding her way and formulating her concepts, viewed the curtailed aspirations suffered by her young heroines as her diatribe against modern civilization. But such a view ignores the full life pattern which evolved in her fiction; for, while the author is obviously sympathetic to her young women, her view of their fate in *Collected Impressions* is clear-eyed: "it is not only our fate but our business to lose innocence, and once we have lost that it is futile to attempt a picnic in Eden" (265). Miss Bowen shares Graham Greene's view that "innocence is like a dumb leper who has lost his bell, wandering the world, meaning no harm." [8] So innocence must not be suffered prolongation; the romantic will must be curbed—and then what? One Bowen character in *The Death of the Heart* summarizes what they all come to see: "Let's face it—whoever is adequate? We create situations each other can't live up to, then break our hearts at them because they don't" (289).

If it is true that every author has only one story to tell and seeks repeatedly for its ideal form, then Miss Bowen's essential narrative begins with the destruction or delimiting of a woman's ideal desires, with her expulsion from a self-defined Eden. She is then confronted with, in Robert Frost's phrase, "what to make of a diminished thing." [9] What she evolves is a mode of living which provides sufficient drama, or occasion to involve and satisfy her lunatic feelings, but which runs no risk of emotional involvement at a level which might entail further disappointment and frustration. This creative activity, which is not engaged in, of course, simply by the protagonist, Miss Bowen terms "art."

A considerable portion of the archetypal Bowen novel is devoted to examining variant forms of this protective artistry. In being defensive and in involving "playing about" to a considerable measure, these created roles remain essentially selfish. In seeking to give an idealistic girl some insight into the whole practice, an older man in *The Death of the Heart* tells her: "What makes you think us wicked is simply our little way of keeping ourselves going. We must live, though you may not see the necessity. In the long run, we may not work out well. We attempt, however, to be more civil and kindly than we feel" (303-4). Another passage in the same novel, recorded by the narrative voice, is even more explicit:

But a man must live! Not for nothing do we invest so much of ourselves in other people's lives—or even in momentary pictures of people we do not know. It cuts both ways: the happy group inside the lighted window, the figure in the long grass in the orchard seen from the train stay and support us in our dark hours. Illusions are art, for the feeling person, and it is by art that we live, if we do. It is the emotion to which we remain faithful, after all: we are taught to recover it in some other place. (111)

A danger to which most of these life-denying art forms are susceptible is the condition of stasis, or to what may be termed "the comfort principle." Once acclimatized to a relatively undemanding role, an individual is content to perpetuate it. Life may not be truly satisfactory, but it is adequate and that suffices. Unlike many fictional protagonists of the last twenty years, Miss Bowen's are not incapacitated by aimlessness; they have a sense of the game they must play in order to survive—and most of them, within its limitations, play it quite well. But their expertise is part of the trouble: it calls for too little effort from them. Several Bowen novels actually commence with their protagonists emotionally more dead than alive.

The Bowen novel begins by attacking youthful emotional ignorance or extravagance, but it concentrates its full force against the twilight security of the pleasure principle. And in this assault Miss Bowen turns the century's mutability to an advantage. Conditions refuse to stay settled for her characters, and sooner or later the unexpected ambushes them. Most of her novels and stories culminate with a moment of shock, a disclosure, or an experience which is sufficiently disturbing to the heroine's emotional being that her formalized role is cracked, increasing the likelihood of a richer, more responsible comportment with life. Miss Bowen stops short of showing the better life, for the achievement of enlarged comprehension and of honest assessments suggests the inevitability of an improved existence—and she will guarantee nothing more.

The highest art in the civilized Bowen world is the practice of "humane manners," which in *Collected Impressions* Miss Bowen terms "the crown of being human" and defines as "the exercise of imagination on other people's behalf" (200). This objective seems modest enough, but her work shows plainly why this art is not readily achieved. All of life, it appears, is calculated to force the feeling person into a defensive position; once assumed, this stance is not readily foresworn. Thus, all of the Bowen novels are structured between two traumatic emotional events: the first discloses the reality of life; the second, the reality of love.

III   *Approach and Style*

In her fiction, Miss Bowen is first of all an impressionistic writer. Since there are degrees of impressionism, she might best be considered a concrete impressionist. Highly selective, she writes a taut, concentrated style which produces clear, well-defined vividness, in opposition to a vague impressionism verging on the dreamlike. Scenes and characters are rendered in few but telling strokes; here, as with other aspects of her work, Miss Bowen's ideal reader is invited to exercise his own imagination and intelligence. She approaches her material nòt as a camera but as an X-ray, and she produces a print of essences from which the reader must create a realistic image.

Miss Bowen tends to "feel" her material—to register it on highly sensitized receptors—rather than to "see" it, as a number of her remarks on writing in *Afterthought* (1962), though not directed specifically at her own work, emphasize: "In writing what is poetically spontaneous, what is most inimitably individual, has this source—the writer carries about him an inner environment which is constant; though which also, as time goes on, tends to become more and more subjective" (208). The nature of the writer's inner being is important in impressionistic writing because, of course, it determines the procedure of selection:

The experience which really influences art does not consist in drama or incidents; it is a sort of emotional accumulation, or, at its best, a slowly acquired deep-down knowledge. Experience is the reaction to what happens, not the happening itself—and in that sense experience is, like environment, to a degree selected. The meaning which is extracted from occurrences varies, and varies in its importance, according to the writer's choice as to feeling: he allows some things to "take" with him more than others. (208-9)

For example, we have in *The Cat Jumps and Other Stories* (1934) a brief description of a room in which several zombie-like characters are about to have a party; we may observe how the author makes us feel rather than see the scene: "A long row of swinging lanterns bobbed in their own horrid light as they pushed open the door.

The lounge was empty and bald as the inside of a band-box, glazed with synthetic panelling. The chairs were askew, empty, with flattened cushions; ashtrays sent up cold fume; the place wore an air of sudden, sheepish vacuity, as though a large party had just got up and gone out. The barman leaned, yawned, just inside the bar shutter" (63).

Miss Bowen's prose is polished and crafted with the care of poetry. But on occasion, however, cutting across the normally elegant surface, like a variation in poetic meter, are deliberate awkwardnesses compounded of syntactical circumlocutions which may remind us of pressurized phrasing by Gerard Manley Hopkins. Here is a brief example of this prose of nervosity, from *Eva Trout*: "Eva, as ever, extra heavily breathing, about to twitch the ignition key" (16). Of language, Miss Bowen has said in *Afterthought* that "[it] can not only register but heighten, by its speed, its emphasis and its rhythm, the emotional pressure we put behind it" (214). Her prose constantly seeks to reflect this pressure of straining suppressed tensions, desires, and emotions. Much is implied, even if little sometimes is seemingly said.

The prose style also relates to the omniscient narrator who writes the fiction. The persona's vision is classical: rational, intelligent, aloof, penetrating, discriminating, and witty; its attitude is humane and benevolent; but it is unsentimental. Its whole approach to life is firm, frank, and wise—what is meant by "mature" at its optimum. Strategically, the mask is most cunningly devised to make effective Miss Bowen's subject—feelings. This threateningly lachrymose topic, in being explored by a convincingly reasonable and open mind anchored by a kind but discreet sense of humor, is accorded relevance, stature, and consequently force. The persona itself becomes an exemplum for a sane handling of the world, as does the one named Henry Fielding in *Tom Jones*. Variation is introduced into the handling of point of view by having the mask merge, when the occasion merits, with a character to express his or her viewpoint. It is a device variously employed for intensity, comedy or irony, or character revelation. There are also times when the omniscient voice draws upon its prerogative to comment directly on characters and circumstances, to link the limited world of fiction to the great world of life.

A very considerable portion of any Bowen novel is dialogue; and it is presented much of the time with only modest intrusions by the narrative voice that allows the reader to gather implication and ramifications. Obviously a measure of obliqueness results, and on this count the author has been accused of obscurantism. Without denying that there are moments when she appears overly elliptical, her technique can be defended. Most directly, her obliqueness serves to make the reader conscious of the difficulties of identifying and assessing the undercurrents of meaning and feeling upon which conversation moves; technique thus functions as a correlative. Furthermore, ellipses are a rich source of suspense and possibility; for, as Miss Bowen observes in *Afterthought*, "the alternatives to the plot, owing to the latent alternatives in the behaviour of the char-acters, must be felt by the reader up to the last moment—it is indeed in this that suspence consists. . ." (219). Finally, the dialogue, which further involves the willing reader in the creative process, enriches and intensifies the whole texture of her work: "In so far as a writer has known more than he says, the reader will in his turn draw from the pages more than is there in print" (217). And, finally, what she has said in defense of imaginative writing, though again not expressed with reference to her own work, is applicable to her fiction: "The work of imagination causes a long, reflective halt in the reader's faculties. It demands to be reread, to be brooded over, to be ingested, to be lived with and *in* (152-53).

In addition to the impressionistic approach, the nervous syntax, the poised persona, and the naked dialogue, two other character-istics are pervasive: a strong sense of place and the play of wit, which evoke a distinct atmosphere. Miss Bowen has said that her fiction frequently originates with feelings arising from a particular locale rather than from a character or a story line. Consequently, her narratives occur in well-realized settings which provide a medium that her characters move through rather than a backdrop for them to perform against. In *Afterthought* Miss Bowen writes, "for me [place and time] are more than elements, they are actors" (96). Some sense of the density of the descriptive passages may be gathered from the following one drawn from her wartime novel *The Heat of the Day* in which descriptions are employed to build up a powerful sense of the exacerbating nature of life in London during the blitz:

In reality there were no holidays; few were free however light-headedly to wander. The night behind and the night to come met across every noon in an arch of strain. To work or to think was to ache. In offices, factories, ministries, shops, kitchens the hot yellow sands of each afternoon ran out slowly; fatigue was the one reality. You dared not envisage sleep. Apathetic, the injured and dying in the hospitals watched light change on walls which might fall tonight. Those rendered homeless sat where they had been sent; or, worse, with the obstinancy of animals retraced their steps to look for what was no longer there. Most of all the dead, from mortuaries, from under cataracts of rubble, made their anonymous presence—not as today's dead but as yesterday's living—felt through London. Uncounted, they continued to move in shoals through the city day, pervading everything to be seen or heard or felt with their torn-off senses, drawing on this tomorrow they had expected—for death cannot be so sudden as all that. (86)

Every Bowen novel employs at least two locales to help establish a moral perspective. In more than one novel a reader may find himself forced to readjust his views of a particular sphere when he realizes its relation to another.

Finally, we need to note Miss Bowen's humor, which usually functions as such only in context; for it is generally of an incidental nature; it is a wry comment or comparison that sparkles for a moment. Some quotable examples are: "her personality was still too much for her, like a punt-pole" (*Friends and Relations*, 22); or, " 'Everyone concerned thoroughly enjoyed themselves, rooting about in their personalities . . . ' " (*The Little Girls*, 207); or, " 'Does it ever seem to you that the non-sins of our fathers—and mothers—have been visited upon us?' " (217). Periodically, Miss Bowen displays her gamin eye at greater length—as, for example, in this passage from *To the North* about a suitable London bus for a young miss:

she had asked Mrs. Patrick, the housekeeper, if it would be suitable for a young girl of her age to go out alone for a ride in a bus. (Pauline had been told what happens in London and warned, especially, to avoid hospital nurses.) Mrs. Patrick, with hospital nurses also in mind, said it depended entirely upon the character of the bus. Taking thought, she had recommended the No. 11. The No. 11 is an entirely moral bus. Springing from Shepher's Bush, against which one has seldom heard anything, it enjoys some innocent bohemianism in Chelsea, picks up the shoppers at Peter Jones's, swerves down the Pimlico Road—too busy to be lascivious—passes not too far from the royal stables, nods to Victoria Station, Westminster Abbey, the Houses of Parliament, whirrs reverently up Whitehall, and from its only brush with vice, in the Strand, plunges to Liverpool Street through the noble and serious architecture of the City. Except for the Strand, the No. 11 route, Mrs. Patrick considered, had the quality of a Sunday afternoon literature; from it Pauline could derive nothing but edification. (58-59)

On the whole, Miss Bowen requires mature readers whose tastes and capacities require substantially demanding work by intelligent authors who are honest in their engagement with the human scene. She is clearly a writer who cannot so much be read as reread. At a time when craftsmanship and high standards become more of an anomaly, Miss Bowen's distinctive tastefulness is to be valued. Edward Sackville West believes she is a writer any advanced civilization would prize; and Miss Bowen is certainly a writer seeking to create the kind of world in which she may endure.

CHAPTER 2

The Sleeping Beauties

> Violence is born of the
> desire to escape oneself.
>
> —Iris Murdock, *The Bell*

Elizabeth Bowen's ten novels may be conveniently divided into three groups because of their central concerns; but the division follows, with one deviation, the natural chronology: (1) her first, second, and fourth novels; (2) her third, fifth, and sixth; and (3) her final four.

What *The Hotel* (1927),*The Last September* (1929), and *To the North* (1932), share is a young heroine who is either experiencing "serious" love or is on the verge of doing so. In each case the women are attractive and intelligent but are emotionally unprepared for the situations in which they find themselves or provoke. When not one of the novels culminates in love, let alone marriage, we have an indication of what the novel of manners has become in the context of this disoriented century. The two girls in *The Hotel* and in *The Last September* are left "free" at the close of the novel; but they are undoubtedly wiser about themselves and the ways of the world, and they are presumably in a position to meet the male sex in reasonable and authentic terms. The heroine of *To the North* finds a solution to her problems in death.

The three books provide a neat progression in their respective relationships between narrative and environment: on the one hand, they move from the most artificial to the most normative milieu; on the other, from the least to the most dramatic or radical story. Thus, *The Hotel* is light in tone; *To the North*, dark. *The Last September* is the most personal, nostalgic, and mellow of Miss Bowen's works.

The three novels present an interesting study in variation. Each story revolves about a "dark" character whose true nature for one reason or another is not readily discernible, and the narrative concludes when this person is illuminated. In *The Hotel*, Sydney's problem is to come to terms, in her own mind, with the figure of Mrs. Kerr; in *The Last September*, Lois must come to see herself. In each novel, visual recognition may in each case be considered as a sign of growth and as a talisman of reasonable expectation. Emmeline's situation in *To the North* is somewhat apart, for she is the mystery in her novel. Her only chance for survival resides in her being seen by someone else before catastrophe strikes; this just fails to happen. The novel's final situation is starkly ironic, for the one person who suddenly understands her is the man who, from her viewpoint, betrayed her; but he sees too late and must pay for his tardiness with his life. Miss Bowen's problem in *To the North* involves the reader directly as the other two novels do not. The reader, like her lover, cannot see Emmeline until the close, which means Miss Bowen must marshal the characterization of her heroine in such a way as to sustain her mystery.

If *To the North* is more successful in individual scenes than in toto, the failure may lie less in the author's execution than in the basic premise that such a problem can yield a successful artistic solution. Miss Bowen's chief aim is to keep Emmeline off stage as much as possible; thus, a considerable amount of talk about her ensues on the part of other characters. Accordingly, this limits the meaningful kind of subjective interplay between sparring individuals which is normally one of the chief delights of a Bowen novel. The book is not without such exchanges, principally between Emmeline and the most interesting of the characters, Markie; but these are minimal. Furthermore, Miss Bowen employs a mirrorlike subplot involving the child, Pauline. These scenes, in themselves pleasing, are heavy-handed insofar as the main story is concerned. The two plots are secured through parallels and contrasts between Emmeline and Pauline, but these prove less than satisfactory because they are so blatant. So, again, the author places herself in a position in which she must forego another of her keenest attributes—subtlety.

Still, whatever its flaws, *To the North* remains a more impressive novel that the author's first, *The Hotel*. Her fourth novel has, as indeed it should, a scenic force and a control absent from the initial one. To begin with, a writer who assembles a cast in a calculated manner and who employs the confines of, say, a boat, an army platoon, or a hotel immediately acquires added artistic obligations.

Despite the seeming complexity created by a disparate collection of individuals and by a temporary context, the reader suspects the author of actually setting up an easy problem capable of dramatic but ultimately of simple solution. Miss Bowen does not really displace these built-in expectations. In her best work the reader's paramount interest arises not from "what will happen?" but from "why is this happening?" *The Hotel* is largely concerned with the question of the second order.

The Hotel has strong affinities with Jane Austen's *Emma*. In each book the heroine overestimates her capabilities, and therein resides the motivation for action; each engages in creating pitfalls for herself. But there are two immediate differences between the novels. Miss Austen creates in Emma a rich character whom the reader may simultaneously laugh at and love; Miss Bowen offers in Sydney a heroine neither likable nor really corporeal and therefore hardly engaging. Again, part of the force of *Emma* results from the closed world in which the characters reside, which means, painfully and deliciously, they must, no matter what transpires, go on living together. *The Hotel* presents an open world, and the tentative nature of the character configurations drain away a great deal of dramatic pressure. The youthful Miss Bowen, who was too ambitious and injudicious with this effort, created among others, the problem of mapping out choreography for an extensive cast. That she manages to do so as well as she does should have been ample forewarning at the time of her future accomplishment. She went on to follow Thoreau's wise counsel, "Simplify, simplify"; and, in due course, she accomplishes much more with much less.

The Last September, the first of the successful novels, skillfully integrates a number of fine characterizations, a movingly evoked world, and a threatening background which licks flamelike along the edges of the scenario proper. Lois comes to life as neither Sydney nor Emmeline does; she is a human being with dimensions in excess of actual story requirements, and hence she escapes the sense of formulation which plagues her counterparts. A number of the people surrounding her likewise have this reverberative quality. Of Miss Bowen's previous characters, perhaps only Markie Linkwater of *To the North* has a resonance equivalent to that possessed by *The Last September*'s Myra Naylor, Hugo Montmorency, and Marda Norton. Here, for the first time, the author employs contrasting settings effectively, which allows the depiction of the army huts to comment upon Danielstown and to evaluate it. This strategy foreshadows the successful use of similar pairings in novels to follow.

I The Hotel

Although Sydney Warren is twenty-two when she comes to spend the winter at the northern Italian resort of *The Hotel* as the guest of an older, doting cousin, she is socially untried and is inexperienced with men. Though little is told of her past, she has been living a no-nonsense, academic life in London and has been seriously considering the study of medicine. By the time the book opens, Sydney has been identified by the hotel's other English guests as an aloof, rather cold, if attractive, person. She has established relationships with only one other individual, Mrs. Kerr, a middle-aged widow. This acquaintance is understandable since Mrs. Kerr is the most polished and knowledgeable of the guests in an assemblage composed chiefly of knitting and bridge-playing matrons. There are the three young Lawrence sisters, but they are vulgarly normal in their concerns with dancing and boys. Mrs. Kerr, who, like Sydney, holds herself above and apart from the others, has taken Sydney in hand as her protégée; and, naturally enough, she flatters her.

Two males enter this world. First comes an Anglican bachelor minister, James Milton, forty, and later, Mrs. Kerr's son Ronald, twenty-two. Approximately in the middle of the novel, James proposes to Sydney; after first being refused, he is accepted. In the closing portion of the book, Sydney breaks the engagements, and the novel ends with James and Ronald, accidentally and ironically, departing together. The other characters, with the season drawing to a close, are preparing for the return to England.

Thus we are most immediately engaged in determining why James comes to propose, why Sydney accepts him and then breaks the engagement and why Sydney and Ronald do not become friends as by rights they seemingly should. Excepting the first of these questions, all of these queries bear upon the relationship between Mrs. Kerr and Sydney, as viewed by the latter. What the reader finally needs to comprehend is the implication of Sydney's angered final remarks to the older woman: "If there's one thing one might hope to learn from you it would be to be sickened and turned cold by cruelty and unfairness. . . . I am very grateful to you;

you have done a great deal for me" (260).

It takes Sydney most of the novel and a considerable measure of anguish and distress to comprehend Mrs. Kerr's true nature. One of the novel's finest touches is its subtle opening scene, for a careful reading of it reveals Mrs. Kerr's self-interest from the start and adds sharpness to Sydney's blindness and gradual awakening. The book opens upon an agitated Miss Pym emerging from an argument with her companion, Miss Fitzgerald. Miss Pym, sick at heart, seeks to bring herself under control when confronted by the imposing Mrs. Kerr and is invited to walk with her toward the tennis courts. Mrs. Kerr sees at once that Miss Pym is upset, but she refuses to be involved in any way: "There were so many things that she might have said just now that Miss Pym could have taken up easily, but she did not say one of them, only exposed with indifference her profile to the sidelong, zealous search of Miss Pym" (15). Mrs. Kerr, aware that Sydney is awaiting her, hurries on oblivious of Miss Pym when they part: "Miss Pym spoke again, louder, but Mrs. Kerr, who was passing through the turnstile, gave no sign of attention" (19). For the present, Mrs. Kerr's elegant, exterior polish hides from Sydney her disciplined feelings, her ability to "[take] fashion in and subdue it and remain herself" (15).

A selfish person, Mrs. Kerr wishes to maintain control over her beautifully performed life, and this desire rules out the possibility of any involvement on the unstable and messy emotional level. Always cordially pleasant, she seeks to see and, so far as it is possible, to place everything in a pleasant light. But, even as a novice novelist, Miss Bowen reveals artistic niceness by refraining from offering Mrs. Kerr as a one-dimensional dehumanized being with a stillborn heart. As a beautiful person, Mrs. Kerr has suffered from problems which confront life's golden children, or at least sometimes appear in their own eyes to confront them. She tells her son: "You see . . . I, who am what is called 'an attractive person,' am going to be lonelier than other people. . . ." When he reminds her that "A large number of people seemed to have loved" her, she replies, "No, no one, I think . . ." (256-57). Because she could be loved readily, she believes she could not be loved well. Her repression of her emotional life began, it may be assumed, simply as self-protection. The word with which she has replaced "love" in her vocabulary and which she employs repeatedly is "fond."

Mrs. Kerr's response to Sydney's anger at the end of the novel cuts two ways. Her "Well, Sydney—what have I done?" is at once a measure of her emotional bankruptcy and a genuine response of surprise to conduct which has been, in her estimate, quite proper. It seems doubtful, finally, that she is sufficiently shaken by the rebuke to embark upon any self-renovation. But the closing encounter is overheard by Ronald; and evidently its substance, prepared for by earlier remarks by Sydney, touches him. He too appears to be "saved" from emotional disenfranchisement.

The early tennis-court scene literally depicts the novel in miniature if the game is equated with life. Mrs. Kerr, who does not play, likes to sit prettily by and watch. Sydney, who has the reputation of being a good player (just as she has a reputation for brilliance), teams up with an older man; but, self-consciously aware that she is being watched by Mrs. Kerr, her game falls apart, and she and her partner are defeated. He feels let down, and Sydney becomes sharp with Mrs. Kerr. Sydney, indifferent to other people, acts almost like a lover toward the fastidious older woman. She suffers until they are together; she is oversensitive in her presence; and she even thinks that, if she does not exist for her mentor as a player or person, she does not exist. It is only necessary to see Sydney with her goodhearted, simple, self-indulgent cousin Tessa (who is almost a parody of Mrs. Kerr) to register the impact that Mrs. Kerr has upon her. Sydney is at least in harmony with the other guests in holding Mrs. Kerr in awe.

Sydney herself is shortly being held in awe by James Milton. James, who goes to a walking picnic organized by Mr. and Mrs. Lee-Mittison without wearing his clerical collar, is flattered first by Sydney's company and then by being included, most gratifyingly, with the younger rather than with the older group of excursionists. Hitherto a confirmed bachelor, James, suddenly caught up in the spontaneity of the younger set, begins to suspect he may have been missing something in life. In his eyes, too, Sydney's poise and apparent maturity make her more desirable and accessible than does the frivolity of her peers. He slowly becomes enamored of her, and proposal is on the edge of his mind whether he recognizes it or not.

Meanwhile, Mrs. Kerr, who has reported the imminent arrival of Ronald, expresses the wish that Sydney and he will become good friends. This friendship which never is realized, though both Sydney and he will come to sense that, under different circumstances, they could have been friends and possibly more. Ronald proves reticent, touchy, and a shade arrogant; and, because of their respective unsettled natures, the events, and the inhibiting near command that they be friends, neither is able to act naturally.

Sydney intuitively gains her first fragile glimmering of Mrs. Kerr when the latter receives a letter from her "little boy." As Mrs. Kerr talks of her son, Sydney detects unnaturalness: "she felt herself beaten back by something that in spite of nature's whole precedent she knew for a falsity; an imposture her immaturity sensed but could not challenge" (99). With Ronald's arrival, Mrs. Kerr plays the part of devoted mother to the hilt; and this role involves the withdrawing of all attention from Sydney, a fortuitous possibility from Mrs. Kerr's viewpoint because of Sydney's increasing pressure on her dormant feelings. Thrown abruptly back upon herself and virtually jilted, Sydney suffers private hurt and public humiliation. It is into this situation James moves.

While he and Sydney are strolling in the neighboring hills, he, as he had no intention of doing, suddenly proposes. Both of them are genuinely startled, but Sydney's automatic response is to refuse him. But by the time they are together again, Sydney has experienced a series of events which cause her to reverse her decision. First, she and a child, Cordelia Barry, have walked past an Italian cemetery and "In such a mood she was not proof against the ordinary reflections on morality as she looked with Cordelia through the cemetery gates" (134). It is, however, less death than "the treachery of a future that must give one to death finally that oppresses her" (135). She is suddenly impressed by James who, she assumes, must have seen her as "ice-bound"; and she sees that his proposal "appeared in the light of present considerations heroic . . ." (136).

Second, Sydney has been confronted by the most dashing of the Lawrence girls, Veronica, who tells Sydney of her own engagement to Victor Ammering, but leads up to it circuitously. Unknowingly, Sydney questions the merit of the bland young man; and Veronica, an extroverted modern young woman, seeks to justify her relations with Victor who has not been popular with the hotel adults. Veronica reveals that Sydney has no copyright on disenchantment, for she tells Sydney: "You see, I've got absolutely no illusions. I do feel I might have been terribly fond of somebody. . . . " She asks Sydney if she "thinks perhaps men aren't what they used to be?" And in a final disclosure adds, "I must marry somebody. You see, I must have some children" (158). Veronica's willingness to compromise her possibilities for fulfillment is rather heady stuff. Sydney is left confronting the vapory nature of happiness: if not for Veronica, for whom then?

Sydney's third and final preparation for engagement has come in a conversation with Mrs. Kerr as they sit in a *patisserie*. After discussing Ronald, they turn to Sydney's "bitterness" over her treatment at the hands of Mrs. Kerr, who comments: "I begin now to guess you've expected much more of me, and that I've been taking and taking without so much as a glance ahead or a single suspicion of what you would want back." Sydney, chilled by this cool analysis, can "only suppose that cruelty as supremely disinterested as art had, like art, its own purity, which could transcend anything and consecrate the nearest material to its uses" (181-82). In the light of these revelations, the engagement becomes both reasonable and desirable. And it might be added that the book Sydney is reading offstage is Thomas Hardy's *Jude the Obscure*.

Sydney's acceptance is an act of cowardice and movement from rather than toward life. She projects the safe, uneventful existence which marriage with James insures; and to her it seems preferable to the ambushes to which her formless life and vague future seem certain to expose her. One of the first to suspect the true nature of the ensuing engagement is, of course, the incisive Mrs. Kerr. In a graciously veiled conversation with James, she causes him to suffer; yet the ambiguous nature of her being leaves the reader wondering whether she is unfeelingly cruel or calculatingly wise. When she says, "her loving you . . . her loving you absolutely . . . ," James grimaces; for Sydney has just admitted to him not only her lack of love but her hope of finding some for him (211). If James, nevertheless, cannot bring himself to break off the affair, he is at least sympathetic with Sydney's feelings when she later announces that she will not marry him.

Sydney must, of course, see into the truth of the situation for herself. The path to this recognition also follows a three-step preparation: conversations with first Ronald and then with James, followed by a motor-car ride along a narrow, twisting road cut into steep cliffs. While out walking, Ronald comes upon Sydney sitting on a rock awaiting James. While they chat, Sydney suddenly becomes aware of the naïveté running beneath Ronald's apparent sophistication; but, more importantly, she recognizes in his views a portrait of herself: "While Ronald talked she often had a giddy sense of watching all she had ever said being wound off from a spool again backwards" (222). When Ronald rises to go, Sydney feels a rush of "panic" and begs him not to leave her alone. Thus, when James arrives, Sydney's emergent uncertainty and her apparent determination to harden herself for her fate causes him more pain. As James listens to her berate happiness, "he could have wept for her . . . " (235). Sydney's final awakening comes in a flash of an epiphany born of shock in a scene which nicely balances the earlier one in the Italian cemetery. While being driven down the steep cliffside road, Sydney envisions the car plunging over the cliff carrying herself, James, Tessa, and Mrs. Kerr to death. When the car has to stop suddenly because the narrow road is blocked, she instantly sees she must go on living. Her earlier sense of life's fleetingness in the graveyard scene is replaced by an insight into its preciousness: "she for the first time felt life sharply, life as keen as death to bite upon the consciousness . . . " (245).

When telling James of her decision, she explains: "I suppose it was the shock of being alive. . . . I had no idea we were as real as this. I'd never realized it mattered so much . . . " (247). It may be seen that Sydney, as well as other of Bowen heroines, has affinities with Sleeping Beauty.

Some critical tears have been shed for James; but these result from a failure to consider his basically robust nature and from the fact that the whole experience opens new vistas of life hitherto unavailable to him. He is quite aware of the truth of her act: "At this moment of the swing apart he was one with her, and was able to say, she is right" (249). Other marriages in the book represent a fate that James and Sydney have most probably averted. The speculative reader might well suspect that Sydney and James would have been similar to the Duperrieres of *The Last September*, Sydney playing Colonel Duperrieres to James's Mrs. Duperriere.

Sydney's act is an affirmation of honest feeling and also a refusal to give up on the vital possibilities of life. Her final anger with Mrs. Kerr, whom she sees as largely responsible for her near entombment, is cleansing; and in turn, it is perhaps restorative for others. In being true both to the society depicted in the novel and to her reading of life, Miss Bowen quite properly leaves Sydney's future tentative. It is evident Sydney is now ready to begin the true, the awakened, ascent of life; but, as for the village at the summit, it "may be deserted." Like Lawrence's *The Rainbow, The Hotel* tells of a girl who has survived a rigorous preparation for adulthood; both novels end by promising no more than promise.

II   *The Last September*

The Last September tells of the last month that Lois Farquar, a nineteen-year-old orphan, spends with her aunt and uncle at Danielstown, one of Ireland's big country houses. It is 1920, the time of the Irish Troubles, of rebels and Blacks and Tans; the sounds of lorries and reports of battle provide the matrix of the action. Lois is another of Miss Bowen's innocents who passes through the twilight zone separating adolescence from adulthood. Introspective and self-conscious, Lois does not know what to do with herself; but, she is most anxious to do something. She asks an older woman, "Did you have any difficulty about beginning?" (136). In the preface she wrote for the novel when it was reissued in 1951, Miss Bowen reveals the autobiographical nature of this question by recalling that she asked herself during youthful summers spent at Bowen's Court, "*what* I should be, and when?" (*Afterthought*, 96).

Initially, Lois's situation does not appear readily promising, located as she is between the moribund Protestant landlord tradition, represented by Sir Richard and Lady Myra Naylor, and the progressively threatening political upheaval. Yet time provides everything necessary for her subsequent two-stage fall from innocence. But the sense of contrivance which marred *The Hotel* is absent in *The Last September*. Miss Bowen is very much at home in this work "which of all my books," she writes in *Afterthought*, "is nearest my heart" (96). The story has a strong sense of dramatic inevitability and unrolls in a vividly evoked world.

Since the story seeks to pinpoint the time when Lois begins to have a life of her own, it is set clearly in the past—the only Bowen novel employing this perspective. This sense of completion is necessary since only in retrospect can we possibly presume to identify turning points or locate significance where, at the time, none was recognizable.

Initially, the run of tennis parties and house guests elicit little more than superficial interest from Lois. Her ostensible beau is one of the locally stationed young English army officers, Gerald Lesworth, who is sincere and gentlemanly but too much the obliging mannequin. Though warmly welcomed at Danielstown, Gerald does not stand high in the estimate of Myra because of his modest background. Lois, wanting to love him, wishes he were more unpredictable and disconcerting; but these qualities he never manages to possess.

Chief among the earlier house guests are Hugo Montmorency and his wife, long-standing Naylor friends. Hugo, once the boyfriend of Lois's mother, is an unhappy individual. A homeless wanderer who moves from visit to visit, he is, in Hemingway's phrase, an arrested adolescent. An introspective dreamer, he has periodically projected big plans for himself; but he has never had the capacity to realize them. Consequently, he is a tense man; and he is touchy because, in his estimate, his position belies his abilities. Thematically, he stands as a warning of what retained innocence can become.

Narratively, Hugo is involved in the first stage of Lois's preparation for maturity. He develops a crush on another Danielstown visitor, Marda Norton, who arrives from England on the verge of thirty and marriage. An attractive creature of sophistication and aloofness, she impresses Lois and prompts her to personal confidences: "Being grown up seems trivial, somehow. I mean, dressing and writing notes instead of letters, and trying to make impressions. When you have to think so much of what other people feel about you there seems no time to think what you feel about them" (136). When she submits her amateurish art work to Marda for comment, Marda tells her it is not good. When Lois retells her egocentric dreams to Marda, Marda tells her: "But be interested in what happens to you for its own sake; don't expect to be touched or changed —or to be in anything that you do" (139). For herself, Marda knows her wisdom, "fruit of her own relations to experience," has been acquired at the price of exhaustion. She regards marriage as a haven that will save her from the wear and tear of existence. But she does remain a capable young woman; quite conscious of her impact upon Hugo, she does not doubt her capacity to handle him.

Lois, Marda, Hugo, and the key themes of violence and awareness merge in a major scene near the close of the second of the novel's three books. The scene witnesses Lois's entrance into a new plane of comprehension. Walking together through a woods, the threesome come upon an old, abandoned mill. Hugo, angered by Marda's playful teasing, settles down on a rock for a smoke and a sulk while the two women push on to inspect the crumbling building. Inside, they come upon and surprise an Irish rebel who has been resting; he points a pistol at them but when they swear silence on the encounter he begins to withdraw. Weak from hunger, however, he slips the gun goes off accidentally, and the back of Marda's hand is grazed. Hugo, who comes running full-tilt, shouts out Marda's name, and a note in his voice strikes Lois more forcefully than has the confrontation with the rebel. Even Hugo, preoccupied with Marda's wound, looks at Lois and has "distantly, some apprehension of an emotional shock" (175). Hugo wishes to dash into the mill but is blocked by Lois and Marda, true to their pledge to allow the rebel to withdraw. Once again angered and feeling exposed, Hugo stalks off. Alone, the women briefly retreat into silence in order to adjust themselves, before Lois says, "I've had a . . . a revelation. . . . I was too damned innocent" (177). The revelation of Hugo's love of which she had been oblivious better serves to acquaint Lois with life in the present. Lois, naturally allowing her mind to drift into the future, suddenly tells Marda: "It's harder, for some reason, to imagine what I'll be doing or where I shall be" (178).

It is appropriate as the novel's third part opens that Lois, with her new sense of alertness, be located for the first time outside her own Danielstown environs. The occasion is a party in one of the huts provided for married army officers and their wives in the nearby village. The raucous, sensual, chaotic scene presents a nice contrast to the Naylor world. This new world is easily accessible to Lois as reality, and here she decides she and Gerald are in love. Not certain where events are leading, Lois thinks, "All the same . . . it is something definite" (223).

Myra Naylor, who recognizes Lois's state quickly enough, is aware that Lois's love is superficial. She tells Lois, "Real feeling explains itself . . . ," and proposes that with autumn approaching Lois go off to art college (231).

Myra then arranges an assignation with Gerald, and her handling of him is dazzling if unfair, for he is no match for her forensic abilities. His inexperience and immaturity are humorously exposed. And, when he draws up his last thrust, "You're not going to stop my seeing her," she replies: "I don't know what sort of girls' mothers and aunts you're accustomed to . . . but how could you expect me to do such a preposterous thing? . . . You know we are always delighted to see you at any time" (250-51). In a state of bewilderment, Gerald himself volunteers as they part, "I promise I won't kiss her" (251).

Myra is one of the finest touches in the book, for Miss Bowen does not allow her to become the stock figure her role in the story implies. A staunch defender of the Danielstown tradition, she suffers from a social narrowness verging on the snobbish; but she is no figure of fun. A robust defender of civilization, she is prepared to act when her high values are threatened. When her home falls at the close, she stands forth stoically as a figure not to be defeated by life.

Gerald meets Lois in the woods of Danielstown for the "frank talk" Marda has urged him to have with her. Lois—already apprised of what has taken place through Francie Montmorency who, ironically has acted "courageously" for the first time in her life in a cause with feet of clay—is more chagrined than hurt that Gerald has meekly accepted Marda's insistence that Lois does not really love him. Her badgering does not convince him: "She watched with agony what seemed to be his indifference" (261). As they part, she may have tears in her eyes, but she maintains sufficient presence of mind to take comfort in the fact that, with summer drawing to a close, the necessity for tennis parties has ended. Earlier, the narrative voice reported that "Lois looked and strained after feeling, but felt nothing. Her problem was, not only *how* to get out unseen, but *why*, to what purpose?" (183). Lois had seen Gerald as her "how," but she had overlooked an answer to the "why." The feelings which have propelled her relationship with Gerald have been mental in origin. When she feels authentically, her ersatz feelings are exposed. Lois, like Sydney before her, comes alive in confronting the reality of death: "Life, seen whole for a moment, was one act of apprehension, the apprehension of death" (277).

Before her impending departure for college, Lois is given a test which permits her to show that she is both able to act upon true feelings, even when she does not feel socially confident, and to defend the standards of her tradition. Unannounced, two silly army wives drive into Danielstown, "shrieking and waving" because they really wish to have a look into the privacy of an aristocratic drawing room. When Lois confronts them she is courteous, nervous, and resolute: "she seemed determined to keep them out" (270). Never having entered the house, the wives leave.

The novel moves swiftly to its close. When word arrives that Gerald has been killed on patrol, Lois accepts the news quietly. Once she had told Marda she would like to act tragically; now, she has her opportunity. Instead, she is very conscious of what the Danielstown people will feel for her and what she will owe them: "She saw that for days ahead she must not deny humanity, she would have no privacy" (276-77). This death, which carries no tragic overtones as the very title of the novel's last part, "The Departure of Gerald," suggests, is taken as the occasion for Lois's own departure into new realms of experience. The reader is simply informed that she has gone to France to perfect her French. That she has not gone to study art may indicate a growth in her capacity for self-judgment —her personal recognition of a lack of talent.

The novel closes with the burning of Danielstown—an episode that completes the simple but profound implication that life consists of loss and gain. In her preface to the novel, Miss Bowen asks, "Was it sorrow to Lois, Danielstown's burning?" (*Afterthought*, 99). The proper answer is surely, "yes, and no." For Marda had once observed that "What Hugo needs is real trouble" (159). The deepest of Lois's feelings belonged to Danielstown; in its loss we are perhaps to read the final touch to her education.

III To the North

Miss Bowen's most dramatic rendering of the dangers of preserved innocence is in *To the North*. In no other novel is she so close to the world of fairy tale as the names of several characters suggest. The imagery identifying the heroine, Emmeline Summers, and her lover, Markie Linkwater, reveals the radical nature of the work; she is likened repeatedly to an angel; he is characterized as satanic and malevolent. She is an "orphan of a dislocated century"; he, a "natural offspring" of it. The novel has been likened to Jacobean tragedy because of its combination of a brooding sense of foreboding and comic byplay.

Critics have regarded the book as a testament to the impossibility for true love in our era. True enough, the novel displays little that is normative; feelings are depicted as either anemic or corrupt, but a less sentimental consideration reveals Miss Bowen as not writing against the age so much as using it to update her age-old problem. She daringly juxtaposes the most idealistic of all her innocents and the most "wastelandish" of all her landscapes, and her point surely is that innocence has never been such a potential liability. Emmeline's apparently deliberate killing of Markie and herself is as much if not more of a comment on her own inhumanity than on the conditions of her environment.

Theoretically, Emmeline has the formula for a rich existence. Publicly, she is willingly in tune with the business of the world— with affairs presented largely through her concern with travel, rail, air, and motor. Emmeline and her partner run their travel agency chiefly on élan, and she loves driving her car. But she chooses to keep her private and subjective lives quite apart from this active public one. The private is to be ordered and mannerly, but the subjective is to be vitally emotional. Though twenty-five, she does not doubt the possibility of an ideal love affair. Emmeline has instinctively an awareness and respect for feeling that Lois Farquar had to discover, but she has not learned as did Lois, the necessity for sharp vision. This fact is pointedly established by her myopic eyesight and by her need to wear glasses. However, he pride keeps her from donning them on social occasions, so that she moves both literally and figuratively through a half world of shadows. Appropriately enough, Markie does not like to see her wearing glasses.

The author develops various ironic situations based on Emmeline's sight. For example, Julian Tower, the man to whom her sister-in-law Cecilia eventually becomes engaged, has an affinity for Emmeline which she cannot comprehend, and which he, because of diffidence, does not press. But the reader is aware he is the very man, as his surname implies, who in his kindness and responsibility would provide her a haven and educate her.

Markie registers with Emmeline because he is different, informal, and humorous compared to the reserved men she knows. He has an emotional current to which she responds, though she is incapable of seeing its superficial, even twisted, nature. Her lack of perception follows the author's having already established how readily Cecilia sized him up on their first encounter. For Markie, feelings are a source of excitement. They are also threatening because, as a son of the century, he suffers from Eliot's "dissociation of sensibility": his feelings are apart from and not subject to the control of the rational mind—"The edge of his mind was restless with superstition: like natives before the solid advance of imperial forces, aspiration, feeling, all sense of the immaterial had retreated in him before reason to some craggy hinterland where, having made no terms with the conqueror, they were submitted to no control and remained a menace. Like savages coming to town on a fair day to skip and chaffer, travestying their character in strange antics, creating by their very presence a saturnalia in which the conqueror may unbend, feeling crept out in him from some unmapped region" (204). An interesting touch is Markie's inability to drive and his dislike of cars; as a sensualist, he naturally abhors what is cold and mechanical. Cecilia claims he has "a Byron complex," and he is characterized as "a voluptuary" (201).

The first half of the novel might be entitled, "Emmeline Triumphant": home life on Oudenarde Road with Cecilia is pleasant and secure; her affair with Markie is inceasingly more satisfying; and the new travel-agency business, with its motto "Travel Dangerously," is a success. Cecilia's Aunt Georgina, fluttering about like a brood hen, is dubious about Emmeline's involvement with Markie but she cannot be taken seriously by either Cecilia or Emmeline since she is forever manufacturing issues: she is "quick to detect situations that [do] not exist" and is prepared to enlarge "her own life in ripples of apprehension on everybody's behalf" (22). Naturally enough this "wolf, wolf," situation contributes to Emmeline's downfall. Cecilia is also rendered more ineffectual in Emmeline's cause by her *idée fixé* that a girl with Emmeline's nature could never love a man like Markie who is such a poseur. Additionally disarming for her intimates is Emmeline's fastidious concern for privacy; for, incapable of distrusting the intentions of others, she cannot conceive of anyone's committing indiscretions against her subjective sense of reality. This penchant for circumspection goes unchallenged because she enjoys the reputation of a sensible girl with a good head for business. In any event, Cecilia notes that the orphaned Emmeline "has done what she likes" since she was twelve (223).

So far as Emmeline is concerned, the climax of her life occurs when her public and private life momentarily coincide. With business flourishing, she and her partner decide to arrange a tie-in with two young men in Paris who also have a small but prospering travel agency. When Emmeline agrees to fly to them for talks, Markie decides he will accompany her for the weekend. In Paris, they sleep together; and, for a brief span, life peaks gloriously; Miss Bowen records this romantic interlude in the most idyllic passages in her fiction. This flight records, however, the height from which Emmeline must crash. The remainder of the novel traces her downward curve.

Actually a crack had appeared before the trip, an incident both forewarning of the future and signaling—or, ironically, failing to signal—the dangers of the unobserved life to Emmeline. She was ambushed when she was alone in the office with the secretary, suitably named Miss Tripp. Coming upon Emmeline, Miss Tripp accused her of heartlessness, implied a considerable fondness for her, and volunteered that she has been dressing for Emmeline. Emmeline is stunned because of her own ignorance of what should have been obvious enough. At the same time, this unsuspected human capacity for perversity comes to her as a revelation. (There is reason to believe her partner, Peter Lewis, is homosexual, something else of which Emmeline is ignorant.) Upset for the afternoon, Emmeline does not transfer to her private life the lesson provided by Miss Tripp. When Miss Tripp is soon replaced by Miss Armitage, the informal and exciting days at the office are numbered. Wonderfully efficient, Miss Armitage progressively takes over until the partners are little more than accessories. Further, Emmeline's private life becomes more troubled, and the travel agency is further dispirited by bad weather and European political tensions.

In the background, Cecilia and Julian have been seeing each other regularly; and Cecilia, though she first hesitates, finally agrees to wed him. Word of the engagement, of what in effect means the impending end of the secure life at Oudenarde Road, reaches Emmeline by telegram at a most inappropriate moment. Hoping to restage the exhilarating Paris weekend with Markie, she borrows a remote sylvan cottage from an acquaintance for a weekend. Envisioning edenic hours with her love, Emmeline makes elaborate preparations to wine and dine him sumptuously. Therefore, she becomes conscious of a change in the atmosphere when, just after they have completed a lengthy drive, Markie insists they backtrack to a village for a meal that Emmeline had proposed to prepare. The romantic cottage, complete with a golden harp, provides an ironic setting for this disclosure of an ailing affair in which she has invested so much of herself. At this time she learns of Cecilia's decision and the weekend is aborted.

Markie returns from the lost weekend to seek out his old, easygoing girlfriend Daisy, an act he has been gradually fomenting. The strain of Emmeline has become too much for him; he has been frightened of her pure, intense, and demanding love, her "exhausting exultation." He feels emotionally incapable of sustaining

Emmeline's golden concept of their relationship. Eventually, her ability to bear his absence crumples, and she calls him. When his telephone is answered by Daisy, Emmeline is chilled and she becomes somnambulistic.

With Hardyesque irony, Cecilia and Julian, at Georgina's insistence, now invite Markie to dinner, for they are unaware of the rift between him and Emmeline. Markie appears and "the incalculable [flares] out,"—he finds himself "ambushed"; for the unforseen beauty" of Emmeline prompts "the violent resurgence of his desire" (312). As Emmeline, at the conclusion of the evening, drives him from London to his destination "to the north," he not only urges her to return with him to his flat, he also urges a return to their former relationship; he even proposes marriage. But Emmeline knows there is no going back: once lost, always lost for paradise. To his importuning, she replies: "And tell the same story again and again and again? There's nothing more left ahead of us" (319). All she now desires is "quiet."

Baffled by her, Markie stares discontently at the dashboard, "at the two lit dials: the clock, the speedometer" (322). Driving furiously, Emmeline seems determined to eclipse both time and space, to move swiftly through the remainder of her life. Markie senses "her speed [has] the startled wildness of flight . . . she [is] like someone who plays the piano wildly to drown some crisis they cannot even admit . . ." (324). She drives "as though away from the ashy destruction of everything" (325).

At the end, Emmeline blames only herself for what has happened and she feels no anger against Markie or the times: " 'One does oneself in,' she said" (322). In one sense, she is right; it has been her own sense of purity which has prevented her from meeting the world on factual terms. But her self-accusation is really the ironic defense of the self-oriented position she has manned throughout. The interconnectedness of life has not registered with her; otherness is beyond her, which is the point of the inset story of the sailor who is moved to kiss her cheek, as well as that of the Miss Tripp interlude. Emmeline is at last to be identified as an narcissist. The repeated emphasis upon her beauty, her passivity, and her eyesight provides the clues to her trouble. Nothing has disturbed her peace; her beauty has been both protective cocoon and sufficient reason for gentle treatment by the passing world. Miss Bowen tells nothing of Emmeline's past because there is nothing to record; she has not had the gradual training which prepares individuals for life's rude and inevitable shocks. Markie, on the other hand—and—this is one of the book's master touches of irony—does progress to awareness and to a greater sense of responsibility toward others. He is capable at the last of self-judgment, of "self-contempt, and a maddening resentment of his desire . . ." (312). Markie, whatever distortions he has harbored, can be seen to have always had the heat of life within. Increasingly terrified by her speed and trancelike driving, Markie speaks her name "hopelessly"; and, "as though hearing her name on his lips for the first time, dazzled, she turned to smile" (327). She, it appears, has already found herself in the promised land and she is joyous to discover Markie's presence. In the instant of distraction, the car plunges head-on into another, killing everyone. The rendering of this last ride together is one of the finest passages in all of Miss Bowen's work.

To the North carries the subsidiary story of Pauline, age fourteen, Julian's ward. Pauline, like Emmeline, an orphan, is not astigmatic. Her growing awareness of the adult world provides a humorous balance to the main plot, as well as a means of placing it. Also like Emmeline, Pauline comes as a visitor to Georgina's country home, Faraways; but Pauline's experiences there are quite different. Surrounded by the human oddities that Georgina has a passion for collecting, Pauline develops her powers of alertness rapidly. She concludes from her experience that "she [will] never feel safe again" (214). Rabbitlike, Pauline is learning she must make her own way in the world; and, conscious of other people surrounding her, she is "anxious to please . . ." (219). She is also capable of sharing a confidence with Cecilia. Pauline, to employ the imagery of the novel, is traveling on a different "line" from that of Emmeline. But Emmeline, in driving "to the north," becomes, in the Lawrencean imagery of *Women in Love*, fulfilled in the frozen reaches of self-love.

CHAPTER 3

The Disruptive Children

> Especially the crimes that spring
> from love seem right and fair from
> the actor's point of view . . . .
> —R. W. Emerson, "Experience"

After leaving her first two heroines, Sydney and Lois, in a vague
limbo following their escapes from false love affairs, it is hardly
surprising that Miss Bowen in subsequent novels explores later
stages of a woman's career. And, with her penchant for young women who entangle themselves with the wrong man, no other variation on her previous stories could be more dramatic than not to
have her heroine escape—what occurs to Emmeline in *To the North*.
In the three novels of the second group—*Friends and Relations*
(1931), *The House in Paris* (1935), and *The Death of the Heart*
(1938)—Miss Bowen continues to explore various consequences
steming from apparently disastrous (in the eyes of the protagonists) early romances. Each book is structured on a pattern of
"before" and "after"—before the disappointment of love and following it. The emphasis in two of the books—*Friends and Relations*
and *The Death of the Heart*—falls upon the aftermath which shows
the heroine, years after being hurt, in each instance coming to terms
with her damaged feelings and painful memories: in so doing, she
gains for herself a more promising relationship with her husband.
The third novel, *The House in Paris*, centers upon the melodramatic early story; it traces step-by-step the young woman's unlikely
and painful self-betrayal.

Miss Bowen's belief in the importance to life of violence continues to manifest itself, but with a new variation. Her earlier mo-
tifs of accident, warfare, and speed are now given human embod-
iment; for each novel includes a child, or childlike persons with
demonic propensities. Ultimately, their disruptive acts rupture the

47

apparently polished surface of life and permit buried feelings to rise and re-energize existence. The three books also witness an evolution of the artistic success of this character. In the first of these *Friends and Relations*, she is poorly integrated into the narrative, and her evenual actions are distressingly arbitrary. In the next, *The House in Paris*, she is less contrived, but in the third, *The Death of the Heart*, she is a perfectly natural function of the story.

These three novels also represent a progression in another way. While the subject matter of these works is intrinsically richer than in the first trio, it presents technical difficulties which Miss Bowen only partially solves. For instance, the tight integration of *The Last September* is missing from both *Friends and Relations* and *The House in Paris*, which have ten-year gaps between the first part of the narrative and the subsequent one. Miss Bowen handles the problem more successfully in *Friends and Relations* than in *The House in Paris*, but not until *The Death of the Heart* (1938) does she manage to regain the esthetic integrity of her earliest work. *The Death of the Heart* is the author's supreme artistic triumph: James Hall calls it "a monument, one of a kind."[1] In a very real sense, it is the consequence and culmination of the author's first five novels.

A third of the way into *Friends and Relations* the narrative jumps ahead ten years to the time when the feelings initiated in the opening sequence which have had a subterranean existence in the intervening years suddenly well up. This great leap forward produces an uncomfortable effect, and the resulting sense of contrivance is never overcome. In retrospect, it appears regrettable that the early material was not introduced into the present story as flashback. *The House in Paris* does begin with the present scene and does raise interest in the causes behind the effects being shown. The lengthy midsection reverts to the past, and then the third part of the novel returns to the present and resumes where the opening section left off. This approach gives the past a sense of drama entirely absent from the corresponding portion of *Friends and Relations*. Still, *The House in Paris* leaves an after-sense of dissatisfaction because the obvious drama of the missing years is never adequately realized and the reader's expectations are not fulfilled. The novel suffers additional difficulties which we later discuss.

The Death of the Heart is the kind of novel an author undoubtedly aims for each time he undertakes one. Every decision seems to be correct, and all of the disparate components are harmonized. The past, the present, and the intervening years are all realized at once in the first third of the novel. The remainder of the narrative is devoted not merely to the laying of a troublesome past but to the emerging issues of the present. Miss Bowen's master stroke is in having two heroines. She combines the story which concerned her in the first group of novels, of first love, with her more recent narrative interest. The younger heroine becomes in this way a correlative for the earlier years of the older one. Actually, the central impact of the story derives less from the outcome of the first love or the confrontation with debilitating memories than from the dynamic relationship of the two women.

The Death of the Heart is an impressive novel in any case; but, when we view it in the context of the author's earlier work, its triumphs even more forcefully impress us. Like an iceberg, five-sixths of the novel bulks beneath the surface.

I Friends and Relations

Friends and Relations opens with a marriage, and a second soon follows. Handsome Edward Tilney chooses as his bride Laurel Studdart, a gentle, attractive Cheltenham girl with a pleasant, low-keyed personality and a true love for her husband. Edward is also loved, and more passionately, by Janet Studdart, Laurel's sister; but not until later in the narrative is the reader apprised of Edward's awareness of his attraction to Janet. In the lengthy introductory wedding scene, the principals are seen only fleetingly: Edward and Laurel as a radiant couple; Janet, as a hard-working organizer. As they appear to the assembled guests, so do they appear to the reader; there are only the barest hints of deeper emotional currents. These, however, register in the unusual mind of an unattractive girl of fifteen, Theodora Thirdman; indeed, much of the scene is observed from her odd point of view.

The daughter of ineffectual parents whom she bullies, Theodora feels bound to make some useful contacts for them since they have recently returned from living in Switzerland and are quite out of touch. Doomed to little success, Theodora does adversely attract the attention of the bridegroom's mother, Lady Elfrida, who calls her "A terrible girl" in response to which Theodora comments to herself, "We shall meet again" (21). And, indeed, they do. With a mind alerted to the deep and the hidden, Theodora grasps not only

that Janet loves Edward but also that Lady Elfrida much prefers
Janet to Laurel. Having ascribed a sense of despair to Janet,
Theodora feels a strong attraction for her.

Two weeks after the wedding, Janet visits friends and meets
Rodney Meggatt of Batts Abbey. Four weeks later, when they
announce their engagement, the immediate repercussions from a
distressed Edward temporarily suspend it. Rodney's uncle, the
explorer and big-game hunter Considine Meggatt, proves to have
been Lady Elfrida's corespondent some years earlier. (It is eventually disclosed that Janet was fully aware of this background
information when she became engaged.) Though a child at the time
of the divorce proceedings, Edward has been scarred by the affair
which saw his mother leave his father, who died shortly thereafter,
even though she does not wed Considine. Edward's near neurotic
touchiness over the whole matter is as expected additionally
excerbated when Janet arrives in London to holiday with Lady
Elfrida, ostensibly to shop for her trousseau.

The first show of feelings between Janet and Edward occurs
at Elfrida's apartment. He accuses her of not loving Rodney; she
retorts that Edward is "like a malicious, horrible child" (72). Only
years later in a soul-searching conversation with Elfrida does
Janet confess the truth that she accepted Rodney impulsively in
order to become really involved with the Tilney family. Janet can
claim only inexperience for her youthful action: "I thought we
might all feel better afterwards; I didn't know it would last. You
see, you see, I had no experience, nothing outside myself" (151).

Two-thirds of the novel takes place, as we have indicated, ten
years following the opening ceremony. The Tilneys now live in
London; Edward works in a Whitehall office; and they have two
children, Anna and Simon. The Meggatts, who live at Batts Abbey
where Rodney conducts a large farming operation, have a daughter,
Hermoine. The families periodically gather at the Abbey; but they
do so only when Considine is absent, which is frequently. When
the narrative resumes, Janet and Rodney are on the verge of a significant decision but do not recognize it as such. It is summer, and
Anna and Simon are vacationing with them. Considine, who is at
"loose ends," is also present; and Janet thinks it would be oppor-
tune if Elfrida were invited to visit as company for him. In defer-
ence to Edward's feelings, Janet and Rodney have never brought
the former lovers together; but now, after all these years, there

seems little reason not to do so if Elfrida will come; and she is quite prepared to do so.

Wishing to act quite openly, Janet writes to tell Edward and Laurel what has transpired, and then she braces for any reaction from London; but none comes. Now another visitor arrives—Theodora. Outwardly, she has grown into an attractive woman; inwardly, she remains the abrasive *enfant terrible*. She decides Batts Abbey is boring, Janet is languid, and the presence of Elfrida and Considine is fascinating. Having looked the situation over thoroughly, she concludes: "I daresay it's time *something* happened" (109). Unbeknownst to anyone, she sends off a letter to Laurel. Shortly thereafter, Edward, maintaining distress at the children's exposure to the corrupt couple, suddenly descends upon the Abbey to claim them. Since the exposure has been in progress for several days, Janet is taken aback. But, in a private discussion, Edward shows Janet Theodora's letter, and it is evident he has been upset by her hints of lovelessness between Janet and Rodney. When Janet says to him, "you need never have come," he replies, "I had to see you . . ." (136). This confrontation stirs their latent feelings for each other, and a showdown between them appears unavoidable. Edward is unsettled and leaves with his children, but a few days later a troubled Janet boards a train for London; she is intent upon talking to Laurel and resolving her own uneasiness.

The events which transpire suggest that the title of the novel's third section, "The Fine Week," contains a pun. The weather is lovely, but events call for delicate handling; and, for a time, Janet and Edward tread very fragile ground. Prior to the trip and while en route, Janet undergoes the Jamesian experience of sensing the presence of a phantomlike alternative being: "a grotesque, not quite impossible figure, had come to interpose between herself and Laurel. A woman, an unborn shameful sister, travestying their two natures, enemy to them both" (173). Janet hopes, in seeing Laurel, to excise this figure. When she does not find Laurel at home, Janet joins Edward for lunch. Inescapably, they meet now "as lovers" (170). Before the day is over, Janet has her talk with Laurel, has Edward to her hotel room, and in the small hours of the morning she returns to the Abbey where she is not expected. Adultery has not been committed, though Edward has tempted it saying, "can't we comfort each other?" (190). Janet, however, refuses.

Evidently, Edward has been attracted to Janet from the first; but,

recognizing her potentially passionate nature, he was afraid of her
—afraid to trust her to the future and afraid too of his own feelings.
With Janet and Elfrida, as it were, on his own doorstep, his skit-
tishness has been understandable. The novel implies a distinction
between love and passion, or the romantic will. Both Janet and
Edward are well loved by their mates; and, even though neither
marriage is in any way passionate, this absence of deep feeling in
no way justifies marital destruction. Janet's explanation to Edward
for her position is brief and to the point: "we have no—no bitter
necessity" (190). Almost defying the sentimental reader to view
her conclusion as simply the truimph of the family over personal
desire, Miss Bowen has Janet play hostess the next day to the Mother's Union.

Edward leaves Janet feeling a great sense of release: "He supposed he must now be delivered from something, free: this term
with no bounds, incapable of appreciation, of measurement, spun
in his head . . ." (210). He is welcomed home by Laurel who has
just reexamined and reassessed her love for him and found it authentic. Simultaneousy, Janet and Rodney, who is innocent of
what has transpired, talk; and, though she makes the remark in
reference to furniture, Janet's comment that "we must reorganize"
says what is necessary.

Faded away again into the background is Theodora, the nemesis,
the saving dark goddess who had acted because she felt Edward
held a "mortmain on Janet's spirit" (112). The attitude of the
Meggatts to her is "fatalistic." Perhaps it is significant that this
strange forceful woman shares a flat with a creative writer. But,
interesting as Theodora is as a character, she is one of the several unsatisfactory aspects of the book. While she conveys Miss Bowen's
sense of the unexpectedness of life and the saving possibilities inherent in it, she functions too neatly as a *deus ex machina*. Miss
Bowen elsewhere is more successful in having her source of shock
spring from her foreground material. Another weak link is the characterization of Edward; for, since we see him almost perpetually
ill-tempered, like a miffed child in the midst of adults, it is hard
to accept as real the feelings lavished upon him by both Janet and
Laurel. And, too, the sensitivity he bears toward his mother's past
is not convincingly explained.

Furthermore, Miss Bowen spends too much time on material that
is too peripheral to the central drama. The long wedding scene,

Laurel's luncheon party, the visit of the Tilney children to the Abbey ultimately are all so much filler. Perhaps the author's decision to tell the story from the beginning instead of commencing with the present scene and slowly disclosing the past was unfortunate. *Friends and Relations* anticipates Miss Bowen's later novels, *A World of Love* and *The Little Girls*, in its concern with buried emotional potential; in each of these later novels, the gradual and fragmented insertion of exposition is employed to intensify the rising drama. No other Bowen novel is so strategically weak as *Friends and Relations*.

II   The House in Paris

The core of *The House in Paris* is the episode in which Karen Michaelis, twenty-three, the engaged daughter of a refined upper-middle-class London family, meets the fiancé of her best friend in Hythe and goes to bed with him. Half of the novel investigates how this affair happened; the other half, divided into two parts as a frame, takes place in the present, ten years later, and records the absorption or normalizing of the earlier event.

The poles of the story are two houses, the Michaelis home in London and Mme Fisher's house in Paris. Karen proves a rebel to the staid, stable home of her parents; Naomi, Karen's best friend, is the reactionary in the unconventional establishment presided over by her mother, the unorthodox Mme Fisher. Karen discovers, finally, the extent to which she is involved in the tradition represented by her family and rushes to embrace it; Max Ebhart, her lover and one of Mme Fisher's emotional captives, discovers that his soul belongs to the older woman and that his only means of escaping her is suicide.

The present occurs on a single day in the Fisher home. Purely by happenstance, Naomi and her now bedridden mother have two young visitors: Leopold, son of Karen and the long-dead Max, is to meet his mother for the first time; the other is Henrietta Arbuthnot, two years older than Leopold, who is being kept by the Fishers as a kindness to her aunt in Mentone whom she is traveling to visit en route from England. She functions chiefly as a means of drawing out Leopold and of providing a contrast to him, particularly in the parallel scenes in which each pays a private visit to Mme Fisher's bedside. The first portion of the book comes to a close when Naomi informs Leopold that, after all, his mother will not be coming to see him. When the present is resumed, the child's stepfather, Ray Forrestier, the man to whom Karen was engaged ten years before, surprisingly arrives in Karen's stead; he spirits the child away rather than have him returned to his foster home in Italy.

Positioned as it is in the novel's structure, Part II abounds with irony. At every step, as Karen ponders the state of her life and moves unknowingly toward her clandestine assignation, she is exposed; she fatefully surrenders to present feelings, misjudges events within the unfolding action, and shows little thought for the future. But her bedding with Max is not so foolish as it may sound in outline. Unlike several other Bowen heroines, Karen is not a completely naïve person; for this reason the situation in which she eventually finds herself is all the more dramatic. The few weeks of her life which are recorded unfold gradually.

When Karen is first seen, she has just entered upon what is to be a lengthy engagement. Her fiancé, Ray, has already bid her farewell and sailed abroad on a diplomatic mission. Their engagement is a widely popular one, and she finds herself subjected to social goodwill to an oppressive extent: "Having to speak of Ray so publicly and constantly began to atrophy private tender thoughts. . ." (69). Her reaction is one manifestation of the sense of depression she has begun to feel toward the society of which her home is representative, "a world of grace and intelligence," where all unpleasantries are "so many opportunities to behave well" (70). She feels chilled by the fixity of her future—by "the world she sometimes wished to escape from but, through her marriage, meant to inhabit still" (71). As a means of temporary relief, she leaves to visit her Aunt Violet and Uncle Bill in County Cork, "the most unconscious of her relations . . ." (69).

Unexpectedly, Aunt Violet troubles Karen as a person who can hardly be said to have lived. When she says to Karen, "One sometimes wishes one had done more," Karen thinks: "Better to be rooted out hurt, bleeding, alive, like the daisies from the turf, than blow faintly away across the lawn like straw" (85). The passivity of Violet's life becomes more of a shock to Karen when her uncle unintentionally discloses the impending serious operation his wife faces. When Karen senses the nearness of her aunt's death, the tentative defiance Karen has been feeling toward her existence becomes bolder; she tells her aunt: "With Ray I shall be so safe..

I wish the Revolution would come soon; I should like to start fresh while I am still young, with everything that I had to depend on gone. I sometimes think it is people like us, Aunt Violet, people of consequence, who are unfortunate: we have nothing ahead. I feel it's time something happened" (87). Since Ireland has made her sense of containment even more acute, Karen is relieved to return home.

In London, Karen finds Naomi Fisher. She has come from Paris to settle a legacy, and with her is Max to whom she has just become engaged, much to her mother's disgust. Glad to see Naomi, Karen tries not to meet Max; but she is forced to do so in the fact of Naomi's insistence. Karen's reticence stems from the period she had spent as a student in Paris living with the Fisher's; for then she had had a crush on Max, a frequent visitor to Mme Fisher's salon; he had wounded her by his failure to so much as acknowledge her existence. In the light of subsequent events, this early revelation of her instinctive fear of facing the realities of the past and her passion to avoid them is instructive. Moreover, Max's cordiality when they now meet, which contrasts to his previous conduct, carries all the greater impact. Looking back later, Karen and Max realize that Naomi has deliberately engineered their confrontation as a test. At whatever cost to herself, Naomi is prepared to learn the quality of Max's affection before the wedding; her deliberate conduct here, as elsewhere, in proceeding carefully helps the reader judge that of Karen.

Karen's nature rises readily to the strange moodiness of Max; since he was the first male ever to prompt strong feelings in her, she chooses to read his attention as a continuation or fulfillment of a time when she seemed to herself a more vital, less self-conscious being. Later, after the seduction, she tells him: "I thought you felt as I did, that this finished the past but did not touch the future. Being here does not seem to belong to now, it belongs to the year in Paris when I used to want you so much even to look at me" (171). Fatefully, Max has appeared at a time when Karen craves drama, as this most telling paragraph makes evident:

She thought, young girls like the excess of any quality. Without knowing, they want to suffer, to suffer they must exaggerate; they like to have loud chords struck on them. Loving art better than life they need men to be actors; only an actor moves them, with his telling smile, undomestic, out of touch with the everyday that they dread. They love to enjoy love as a system of doubts and shocks. They are right: not seeking husbands yet, they have no reason to see love socially. This natural fleshly protest is broken down soon enough; their natural love of the cad is outwitted by their mothers. Vulgarity, inborn like original sin, unfolds with the woman nature, unfolds ahead of it quickly and has a flamboyant flowering in the young girl. (112)

In the weeks following Max's departure from London, Karen asserts her desire to wed Ray; but a new note has now been introduced to her future: "her thoughts had bent strongly to whatever in marriage stays unmapped and dark, with a kind of willing alarm. She had now to look for Max in Ray" (130). Then in succession come a telegram, a letter, and a phone call. The telegram announces the death of Aunt Violet; as with Sydney Warren's graveyard scene in *The Hotel*, the presence of death prompts in Karen not only a sense of transitoriness but the need to grasp life immediately. The letter from Mme Fisher to Mrs. Michaelis is an odd, unexpected one; Karen, pondering over it, puzzled, wonders why it was written. Her astute mother sees the key point (though she too shakes her head at what she takes to be the strange ways of the French). In the letter, Mme Fisher suggests that Max is marrying Naomi simply because of her newly inherited wealth. In her own way, Mme Fisher is beginning to clear the way for an engagement between Karen and Max. When Max then phones Karen proposing a rendezvous in Boulogne, she agrees. In the channel port, Karen learns why Max has called : he tells her that he has heard from Mme Fisher "what [he] dared not think"—namely, that Karen loves him (140). Karen does not deny this, but they both agree they can never marry. Max grants that he needs Naomi; Karen simply decides that she can no longer go through with her marriage to Ray. This decision has the effect of rationalizing the possibilities for her present conduct. When Max tells her that she should go home, that she really does not want adventure, she asks, "Why else am I here?" (155). They then agree on a weekend at Hythe.

Though ample evidence is available, Karen ignores or denies two facts about Max. The first is that Max is in love with her, which she knows for a fact in Hythe. Apprised of it, she says feebly, "I didn't know. . . ." Max answers, "You force me to hide myself." and Karen adds, "If I had known you loved me I would not have dared come" (176). The second fact is that Max is unstable; he himself has been quite insistent about his capacity for erratic behavior. When, in due course, Karen receives the telegram from Naomi reporting Max's suicide, the truth of this instability is fully borne out.

The cause of the suicide stems from Max's realization that he has not escaped the will of Mme Fisher as he had assumed. In her reaction to his news about his affair with Karen, it becomes clear to him that, far from acting independently, he has simply been carrying out her desires. This coincides with the distress he already feels over the troubles Karen faces at home. As Naomi later explains to Karen, "I saw then that Max did not belong to himself. He could do nothing that she had not expected; my mother was at the root of him. I saw that what he had learnt about you and him pleased her, that she had pleasure in it in some terrible way" (194). Namoi then adds that Max was finally crushed by the awareness that "his love for [Karen] had fallen into her hands" (195). Max's only means of escape, his only means of revenge against his captor, was suicide. However, Naomi insists, it was not a calculated but an emotional act—an act of passion.

Her lover gone, Ray in all probability lost, and, with child, Karen tells Naomi: "In ways, you know, Naomi, I should like very much to be ordinary again" (200). Her reaction to her adventure in fact proves total; for, when Mrs. Michaelis dies shortly after the suicide, in effect having been killed by her daughter's conduct, Karen seeks to emulate her completely. When Ray returns, he takes everything in stride and sets aside his diplomatic career for what proves to be a lucrative one in business in order to wed Karen. The child Leopold, the leftover past which Karen no longer wants, finds sanctuary through Naomi's efforts with a wealthy but childless American couple. Whether or not Karen could actually have exorcised the child from her mind is an academic question since Ray keeps the fact of Leopold's existence alive, not in any way vindictively as a threat held over his wife, but in his desire to accept all of Karen and out of a sense of responsibility toward Leopold. Ray has waited patiently for Karen herself to want the child, or he has waited patiently until Karen is unable to meet her son at the house in Paris. Finally, having acted, Ray does not know how Karen will react to his possession of her son; the reader suspects that Leopold's ten-year journey to his Ithaca is accomplished.

Leopold, true son of Max, appears as a high-strung, introspective, complex child. His adjustment to new circumstances, it may be judged, will not be easy; for he is unlike his Paris companion, Henrietta, who is already conscious of adult conduct and of the world as a trying place which must be taken in stride. Ray Forrestier appears, however, to be the man most likely to succeed with Leopold. Hardly wishing to leap out at Leopold on their first evening together, Ray confines his thoughts to himself; they will be expressed soon enough: "(. . . You will notice, we talk where I can talk. You will not quote Mme. Fisher, you will not kick me in taxis, you will not shout in houses where they are ill. You will wear a civilized cap, not snub little girls and not get under my feet. There will be many things that you will not like. There are many things that I do not like about you.)" (255-56). At the close, Leopold is like "someone drawing a first breath" (256).

The House in Paris enjoys considerable critical esteem. Artistically, everything which is introduced into the novel is "used"; and it must be granted that the execution fulfills the concept. However, various aspects of the work lead me to rank it lower than other critics. First, the dramatic irony of the second section becomes so repetitive it finally has an adverse effect upon the reader, for the author appears to be scoring points off her heroine all too easily. Irony employed this relentlessly must yield to a large illumination or prove humanly aggrandizing in order to justify itself. But this irony achieves no such end.

Second, while the characterization of Leopold is quite convincing, far too many pages are devoted to him. He is presumably what the story demands he be—a complex, unhappy child with a troubling mixture of innocence and astuteness. But the points that need to be made regarding him could have been made more succinctly. Clearly Miss Bowen wants him to be taken seriously. When, for example, Naomi comes to take him away from his visit with her mother, she says, "You must come now, at once. I have left you here too long" (223). This remark is intended to carry threats of danger and corruption, but it is hard to be deeply concerned with a nine-year-old who can hardly be credited with comprehending the rebellious philosophy being expounded by Mme Fisher.

And, third, serious doubts must also be raised about the whole relationship between Mme Fisher and Max. It strikes a note of strident melodrama, and it remains an unconvincing solution to the artistic problem of finding a means for Karen to stumble into a painful experience and bear a child. Fourth, and finally, the reader is left with a sense that Miss Bowen ignored the potentially richest portion of her story in the return of Ray from the East, his subsequent marriage to Karen, and their living "without" Leopold.

There are fine things in the novel, not the least of which are the characterizations of Naomi and Ray. Very near a nonentity in personality, Naomi could have been a flat-stick figure while in fact she is well and humanly realized. And Ray is a minor triumph for Miss Bowen who is always stronger in creating women. Though his part is small, he comes fully to life.

III   The Death of the Heart

No Bowen novel has a more comically dramatic opening situation than *The Death of the Heart*. Into the adjusted, unemotional, childless, eight-year marriage of Anna and Thomas Quayne drops Portia, age fifteen, Thomas's half-sister. The Quaynes open the door of their expensive, overly ordered Regent's Park home with little enthusiasm to this newly orphaned child who was conceived in adultery. They are somewhat sustained by the possibility she may be shifted to other realatives after they have had her a year as the elder Mr. Quayne has beseeched them to do. The narrative culminates in a series of shocks: Portia is galvanized into action which, in turn, rebounds upon the Quaynes. By the end of the novel, considerable readjustment at 2 Windsor Terrace seems to be in the offing, and Portia's visit is quite likely a permanent one.

Though much of this "double-stranded" book records Portia's growth and her necessary loss of innocence, the more basic issue is the revitalization, perhaps simply the vitalization, of the moribund marriage. Much of this novel's brilliance results from the skillful blending of these two concerns and their subsidiary matters. This is Miss Bowen's most successful novel, artistically and commercially; and, along with *The Heat of the Day*, it constitutes the peak of her achievement.

The Quaynes have been living more of an arrangement than a marriage, for each came to it as an emotional cripple. Anna wed on the rebound from the one great love of her life, Robert Pidgeon. Though he dropped her, she has never come to terms with this romantic interlude; she harbors Pidgeon in the recesses of her mind in the same way that she has his letters secreted in a secret drawer of her desk. From her viewpoint, Thomas offered a quiet, undemanding, comfortable marriage, largely because of his passionless nature.

Her hopes of establishing a normal role as a mother have long since vanished with her failure to terminate her pregnancies: her disappointment and her consequent adjustment to childlessness contribute to her stiffness toward Portia. She has settled down to find satisfaction in safe male admirers who can entertain and flatter her but who require no physical reward. Three such bachelors are on the scene during the course of the novel: St. Quentin Martin, an urbane novelist; Eddie, a bright young man employed at Thomas's advertisng agency; and latterly, Major Brutt, an older gentleman, a friend of Pidgeon, and recently returned to England and out of touch. As with several other characters in the novel, Anna's appearance belies her inner being; for beneath her brittle sophistication lies an insecure woman who has never risked much for fear of being something less than the best. She is a dabbler.

Thomas originally wed Anna because she was pleasant, self-possessed, and seemingly unconcerned with emotion: in short, she was an ideal marital companion for a man who found the opposite sex a source of anxiety and who abhorred thoughts of intimacy. Marriage for both partners, then, came as a source of relief and as an opportunity to live a quiet life. However, following the ceremony, Thomas experienced the unanticipated; he fell passionately in love with Anna; but assuming her allegiance to their tacit agreement of quietude, he suffers his pent-up feelings privately. In Bowen terms, both are failing to exercise their full emotional potential and will not likely do so unless their current roles are altered. Clearly, this function is to be played by Portia.

The story opens upon Anna and St. Quentin strolling in a winter landscape. She tells him she has been reading Portia's diary which she came across accidentally, for Portia's record of her days at 2 Windsor Terrace has quite unsettled Anna. It is, she says, "completely distorted and distorting. As I read I thought either this girl or I are mad" (13). Portia has seemingly missed nothing, though "There's certainly not a thing she does not misconstruct" (15). Standing on a bridge in Regent's Park, "their figures sexless and stiff," Anna and her companion watch swans "in slow indignation" swim down cracks in the frozen surface of the lake" (10). Fittingly, Portia becomes associated with bird imagery; and her initial condition is not unlike that of the swans. Because Portia does not learn of Anna's acquaintance with her diary until Part III of the novel, repercussions do not come until then. Most of Part I is devoted to characterizing life at Windsor Terrace and to explaining Portia's background.

When Portia's father, the senior Thomas Quayne, was fifty-seven, he had "lost his head completely" and had begun an affair with a woman named Irene, twenty-nine (22). As Anna explains his situation to St. Quentin: "He and [Mrs. Quayne] had married so young— though Thomas, for some reason, was not born for quite a number of years—that he had almost no time to be silly in. Also, I think, she must have hypnotised him into being a good deal steadier than he felt. At the same time she was a woman who thought all men are great boys at heart, and she took every care to keep him one" (13-14).

Mr. Quayne is another instance of retarded adult innocence and of the need, at whatever the risk, for youthful excess. When Irene becomes pregnant, Mr. Quayne tells his wife; and "Mrs. Quayne [is] quite as splendid as ever . . ." (23). She becomes "all heroic reserve," calms her husband, packs him off to Irene, starts divorce proceedings, and settles down to enjoy her house and garden in contented peace. Like hopeless babies, Mr. Quayne and his bride retire to the south of France and begin a wandering existence in cheap hotels. He suffers because the growing Portia has no proper life; and during a trip to London, he secretly inspects Windsor Terrace and envisions his daughter sharing the normal family life it suggests to him. After he dies, Portia and her mother continue the transient existence; but, when Irene suddenly dies after an operation, Portia becomes her father's legacy to Regent's Park.

An inside view of the Quayne affair is provided by an older servant, Matchett, who had worked for Thomas's mother before coming to Anna along with her mother-in-law's good furniture when she had died. Matchett, stolid and humorless, but Portia's only source of affection, makes a distinction between the right action and the good one. In her view, Mrs. Thomas Quayne "meant to do right" (95). She explains to Portia, "Sacrificers . . . are not the ones to pity. The ones to pity are those that they sacrifice" (90). She has been a great admirer of Portia's father who, in her estimation, was unlike his wife in being honest and natural. She views Mrs. Quayne as a role player who was prepared to maintain her concept of herself at whatever cost to anyone else. In the light of Matchett's views, we see that Thomas and Anna are also doing the "right" rather than the good thing by Portia.

This background detail helps to account for Anna's report that she and Portia "are on such curious terms—when I ever do take a line, she never knows what it is" (11). Quite evidently, feelings must come to replace manners. That Portia, however, has two left feet because of her inexperience is humorously brought out in scenes at her private school for girls where she is decidedly unsuccessful in coping with the established decorum: "she had not learnt that one must learn . . ." (65). Small wonder she feels all of London threatening her:

> She had watched life, since she came to London, with a sort of despair— motivated and busy always, always progressing: even people pausing on bridges seemed to pause with a purpose; no bird seemed to pursue a quite aimless flight. The spring of the works seemed unfounded only by her. . . . She could not believe there was not a plan of the whole set-up in every head but her own. . . . nothing was not weighed down by significance. In her home life (her new home life) with its puzzles, she saw dissimulation always on guard; she asked herself humbly for what reason people said what they did not mean, and did not say what they meant. She felt most certain to find the clue when she felt the frenzy behind the clever remark. (72-73)

Having a modest relationship with Anna and Thomas, and a closer but milder one with Matchett, Portia grabs rather eagerly at the interest shown in her by the irresponsible Eddie. From the viewpoint of the contemporary British novel, Eddie is an interesting creation because he so evidently anticipates Kingsley Amis's Lucky Jim; for, like him, Eddie comes from a modest background and is seeking to locate himself in the Establishment, in which he does not believe. A very conscious role player, Eddie prefigures Lucky Jim in his habits of face making and mimicry.

The relationship between Portia and Eddie is undemandingly comfortable from his viewpoint. He takes joy in her childlike innocence, and he feels she is the one person with whom he need not assume an interminable pose. Eddie, as it develops, misjudges in assuming that Portia will place no demands upon him. Really a very self-centered being, he is concerned with his welfare and personal freedom; but his surface superciliousness really cloaks despair. An "experienced innocent," Eddie bears a resemblance to Emmeline of *To the North* in his unwillingness to adjust to the nonedenic facts of life, or at least in his unwillingness to adjust without exacting his own price from the world. He seeks to punish and to travesty love because it cannot be what he longs for it to be; he sees only himself as reality since he is the only person he is prepared to trust. Portia, from his viewpoint, is really a new lease on the impossible life; with her, he seeks to sustain the innocence of adolescent love, the state which holds out to him the possibility of beautiful fulfillment so long as it is never tested. Portia, of course, has no such insight as his; but she discovers soon enough Eddie's unwillingness to allow their affair to progress, and she is left pondering his distress over her unwillingness to sustain their status quo and her desire to grow up.

Part II, "The Flesh," shifts to a contrasting setting, one which offers Portia an alternate kind of life with its own range of new characters and experiences. Anna, feeling the need of a vacation, whisks Thomas to Capri; Portia is sent to the seaside at Seale to live with Anna's one-time governess, the widowed Mrs. Heccomb and her two working step-children, Dickie and Daphne. Home is called Wakiki (which is intended to give this sequence overtones of undemanding, irresponsible Pacific Island life), and the household is the antithesis of the highly mannered Windsor Terrace. Wakiki is sustained by blasting radios and by conversation conducted by shouting above them; all is "pushing and frank," though neurotically proper. Portia discovers "the upright rudeness of the primitive state—than which nothing is more rigid" (207). Life at Windsor Terrace is "edited," but that at Wakiki is the reverse. The contrast recalls that between the stately home in *The Last September* and the huts of the army families.

More at home at Wakiki but still reticent, Portia falls in with the crowd presided over by Daphne and Dickie. Portia soon becomes anxious to invite Eddie for a weekend; and Mrs. Heccomb, assured that Eddie is well known to Anna, assumes his visit will be quite proper. Portia awaits his coming anxiously, for she has decided on the reality of Seale and wishes him to confirm it for her. Eddie has hardly arrived, however, before he declares it "unreal"; for in his self-conscious state he is well aware Wakiki is the unexamined life. The only member of the Seale crown who is at all introspective is barely tolerated—is considered ineffectual and labeled "a cissie."

Unknowingly betrayed in London by Anna, Portia is to know betrayal in Seale through Eddie. Sitting between Portia and Daphne at a Saturday night movie, Eddie ends up, as Portia discovers, holding Daphne's hand. Since Eddie has been introduced into the crowd

as Portia's friend, she finds this experience painful. When she is
alone with Eddie the next day, she challenges his conduct. The
episode, he explains, is innocent enough in his view and was intended to lead to nothing further; but this view is not easily conveyed to Portia. In fairness to Eddie, it must be said that he has
warned Portia not to get serious with him and to make demands:
"Never *be* potty about me: I can't do anything for you" (256). Furthermore, Eddie anticipates what St. Quentin later elaborates for
Portia when he says, "Don't you know how dreadful the things you
say are?" (257).

In her diary Portia views Seale to London's disadvantage: "In
London I do not know what anybody is doing, there are no things I
can watch people do. Though things have hurt me since I was left behind here, I would rather stay with the things here than go back
to where I do not know what will happen" (274). Even Portia feels
the great temptation of comfort, of seeking out an effortless stasis.
However, she must return to London to be greeted by Matchett,
who observes, "I can't see that this change has done you harm. Nor
the shake-up either; you were getting too quiet" (280).

When Thomas and Anna return, it is evident they have not
changed. Having been greeted warmly by Portia in the front hall,
Anna cannot wait to go up to her bath; and Thomas, claiming a
headache, quickly vanishes into his study. Later, Thomas observes
to Anna, "Portia gave us a welcome"; and she replies, "It was we
who were not adequate." But Anna remains prepared with her
justifications: "let's face it—whoever is adequate? We all create
situations each other can't live up to, then break our hearts at them
because they don't" (289). This statement proves a telling one in
the light of ensuing action. Though aware of their inadequacy in
dealing with Portia, the Quaynes seem prepared to let matters
drift. In the Bowen world, they are riding for an upset.

Critics generally agree that the "devil" of the final section is
St. Quentin since he imparts to Portia the "forbidden" knowledge
that Anna has been reading her diary. However, the devil may more
properly be viewed as a situation rather than a person; for a comment Major Brutt makes to Anna provides the clue: "that's the devil, you know, about not having a fixed address" (315). This statement assesses the root of the trouble, for what Portia ultimately
feels is a lack of any sense of permanency. Her efforts at the close
are directed toward finding a sanctuary; and, in a rather roundabout

manner, she probably succeeds.

After learning from St. Quentin of Anna's having read the diary, Portia telephones Eddie to tell him, and he in turn calls Anna; and, though his position with both Thomas and Anna is insecure, he conveys his displeasure. When five days later, Portia arrives home to find Anna and Eddie tête-à-tête over tea, she is convinced they have been talking and laughing together about her. Two days later, when Portia walks out on Windsor Terrace, the time lapse, observes the narrator, is "long enough for the sense of two allied betrayals to push up a full growth, like a double tree . . ." (327). Portia leaves her home after having arranged to meet Eddie; and, unbeknownst to him, she is intent on living with him. After Eddie has been more or less forced into taking her to his apartment and after he has reiterated his earlier claim that she does not know the ropes and has "a completely lunatic set of values" and that he simply cannot risk harboring her, she departs prepared to play her final card. She goes to Major Brutt, tells him she has "nowhere to be," and informs the poor dazed man that she wishes to marry him. She rather cruelly seeks to enlist him as an ally by telling him that Anna also laughs at him. When he insists that he must call Windsor Terrace, Portia tells him that Thomas and Anna will not know what to do; and she instructs him to say that her return will depend on their doing "the right thing."

Meanwhile, Portia's absence has been noted by the Quaynes and St. Quentin, their dinner guest. The air is already tense, and Anna and Thomas have already begun unburdening themselves to each other when the Major's call comes. Thomas now learns about the diary, and the scene which this disclosure threatens is just barely avoided as they turn their attention to the question of "the right thing." They quickly enough reject any thoughts of having Portia come across town alone in a taxi or of her being escorted home by Major Brutt. The importance of the issue they do not doubt; Anna points out: "It's not simply a question of getting her home this evening; it's a question of all three going on living here . . . yes, this is a situation. She's created it" (371).

When St. Quentin initiates an important train of thought by suggesting that Anna and Thomas "are both unnaturally conscious of [Portia] . . ." (372), Anna seeks to put herself in Portia's place and to express what her feelings must be: "Frantic, frantic desire to be handled with feeling, and, at the same time, to be let alone.

Wish to be asked how I felt, great wish to be taken for granted—"
(377). The right act, really the good act, the natural thing, they
decide is "something quite obvious. Something with no fuss" (375).
When Portia is normally brought home, Matchett brings her; so they
dispatch Matchett and also decide against calling Major Brutt.
Thomas says, "This is a *coup* or nothing" (377).

Miss Bowen implies in her closing passage that life at Windsor
Terrace will be better, but she once more avoids suggesting any
miraculous change. Anna has already shown a humanitarian side,
one that Portia is unaware of, in her efforts to find employment
for Major Brutt, whose worth she recognizes. And she has also and
most importantly come to terms with her harbored past feelings
for Pidgeon. She admits to herself, as she never previously has,
and tells Major Brutt as much, that Pidgeon did not really care
for her, that their affair came to nothing because neither trusted
the other. And she and Thomas have talked, as Thomas earlier com-
plained they never did. Having "saved" Portia by pulling her back
from a speeding car on one of their recent strolls in the park, he
now appears committed to saving her in another sense. Emphasized
at the very close, and clearly intended to contrast with the frigid
landscape of the opening, is a description of the spring evening
with its "intimation of summer coming . . . " (384). And the piano
music issuing from an open window as the curtain falls hints at the
new harmony seemingly to be realized at Windsor Terrace.

CHAPTER 4

The Power of the Past

> Remember that all our failures
> are ultimately failures in love.
>
> —Iris Murdock, *The Bell*

Miss Bowen's third group and final four novels disclose her readiness to set herself new and challenging problems. In part, of course, she had to move on from *The Death of the Heart*, which carried her earlier material to a finely realized logical conclusion. Aside from this novel, her last work is in many ways her most interesting; for it shows the author working with a new sense of adventuresomeness. And, if none of these novels quite match the perfection of *The Death of the Heart*, they reflect the touch of a poised and knowing craftsman. *The Heat of the Day* (1949) is the most ambitious of her novels; *A World of Love* (1955) and *The Little Girls* (1964), her most intellectually intricate; and *Eva Trout* (1969), the most bizarre.

The Heat of the Day, which is set chiefly in wartime London, aims to make a major statement about the conditions which preceded and fomented World War II. In addition to being a professed "big" novel, it is Miss Bowen's most daring one. As such, it has vulnerable aspects which some critics have readily noted. In this novel, as in no other, the characters function symbolically; they stand for classes of people and social tendencies as Miss Bowen saw them function between the wars and fulfill themselves in the holocast. In outline, the central love triangle, composed of a woman who has abdicated the artistocratic responsibilities of her class and two men who are a spy and a counterspy, appears improbable and melodramatic. But, if the threesome is viewed as moving through the dense wartime milieu with its pervasive sense of exaggeration and unexpectedness, the improbability is lessened. The heroine, in spite of the significance she must bear, is possibly the best realized one in the author's gallery.

A World of Love is the one instance in which Miss Bowen's style assumes a disproportionate importance. The verbal preciousness is distracting, if not finally destructive, since it creates difficulties of comprehension which are out of all proportion to the worth of the subject matter. Like *To the North*, *Friends and Relations*, and *The House in Paris*, this novel is a work with parts rather than a whole piece. Considered in conjunction with *The Last September* and *The Death of the Heart*, however, *A World of Love* affords an interesting combination and a reworking of previous material toward a new realization. It shares with *The Last September* an Irish setting and insights into the Irish character; like *The Death of the Heart*, it employs more than one heroine. As a literary performance, *A World of Love* is clever; to make any additional claim for it is difficult.

The Little Girls, like *The Heat of the Day*, is symbolic; but it differs in the degree of ambivalence attached to its symbols. Consequently, this novel is Miss Bowen's most challenging book; this fact is all the more surprising in the light of its taut and racy style. We might conceivably be reminded of Wallace Stevens's poetry with its pure, crystalline exterior and its metaphysical interior. In this novel, the author presents what must constitute the ultimate variation upon her innocent heroine character by creating one who is sixty-one years old.

By virtue of the emphasis in these three novels upon the past as it impinges upon the present, these novels constitute a group. The topic is one that has always interested Miss Bowen, but it is one which she had not previously dealt with so pervasively or so radically. Compared with her other books, these quite simply encompass more time since most of the principal characters are older: those in *The Heat of the Day* are around forty; those in *A World of Love*, over fifty; the women in *The Little Girls*, in their sixties.

These books emphasize that the quality of an individual's life is significantly influenced by his attitude to his accrued memories and experiences. Characters in each of the stories are shown in the midst of life as acting upon distorted and delimiting recollections, and they are forced by circumstances to confront this fact. Thus they are afforded an opportunity for reassessment and readjustment toward a more vital existence.

Eva Trout is somewhat apart in arriving at a negative conclusion. It too shares a concern for the past, but the heroine, rendered permanently inept by a careless upbringing and burdened with inherited wealth, is unable to gain self-knowledge or an achieved life. Miss Bowen's last novel is her weirdest and darkest.

I   The Heat of the Day

Miss Bowen's one attempt at the big novel, *The Heat of the Day*, is her most powerful one; but it is not so perfectly realized as *The Death of the Heart*. Nonetheless, these remain as the twin peaks of her work. Described as both a war novel and a love story, the novel is either only in a limited sense. The impact of the war, particularly the bombing of the civilian population of London in 1942, is tellingly rendered. But Miss Bowen is not interested in the war per se; rather, it is presented as the logical culmination of the between-the-wars wasteland. The war, then, while vividly real, an undeniable actuality, is employed poetically or imagistically and with no regard for actual history.

Prewar conditions, conveyed through the lives of a handful of characters, are analogous with the social situation in any other Bowen novel—situations which, as previously noted, have their own counterforce built into them. As one character observes, "Dunkirk was waiting there in us . . . " (263). With a situation so radical as a war, it is not feasible to postulate recovery for the generation for whom the landscape of blitz is an inevitable inheritance; with the war comes an exhilarating release from the torpidity of the wasteland, but the forces of shock, having to be extreme, are largely self-destructive. In a book, however, which regards the war as a social watershed, it is appropriate that there be the subsidiary theme of the fresh start and that it be expressed through members of the new generation which will inherit a world cleansed by the massive convulsion.

No Bowen novel suffers more from story summary than this one; indeed, some of its melodrama must needs sound incredible. But, as we have observed, the heightened wartime atmosphere serves largely to absorb the melodramatic incidents. Few readers would deny the author gains a "willing suspension of disbelief." The central story revolves around Stella Rodney, a handsome woman in her forties; her lover Robert Kelway; and her would-be lover, Harrison, a skulking counterspy. Stella is a relatively normal character, but the two men are aberrations. Stella and Robert, both engaged in secret government work, have been in love for two years.

Harrison, a man Stella has met only once previously, contacts her claiming urgent business and comes to her flat. He has two pieces of information and a proposition to make her: first, Robert Kelway is passing information to the enemy; second, only he, Harrison, knows this fact. His proposition is quite to the point: if Stella will become his mistress, he will not report Robert. Clearly, this situation has all the makings of a Graham Greene novel with its usual atmosphere of seediness, but Miss Bowen's treatment is quite different. The reader is surprised that Stella's reaction to Harrison is not considerably sharper than it is; but not until near the end will he come to understand the calmness of her response. Quite obviously the book begins with very strong appeals to the reader's curiosity. The odd nature of Harrison, the truth of his accusations, and Stella's reaction are all to be wondered at.

Early commentators recognized that *The Heat of the Day* has affinities with E. M. Forster's *Howards End*. In his novel, Forster draws into contact representatives of the three broad classes of English society: Margaret Schlegel, middle class; Henry Wilcox, upper class; and Leonard Bast, lower class. Miss Bowen offers Stella and her son Roderick as representatives of the upper class; Harrison and Robert of the middle; and, the principal character of an important subplot, Louie Lewis, of the lower. In a comparison of the two novels, William Heath makes this most useful observation: "the distance between their final attitudes can suggest a great deal about the forty-year period that separates [them]." [1]

For Forster, the Schlegels represent the hope for a healthy society, the responsible balance between the "prose" of public demands (the overly abstract Henry) and the "poetry" of private need (the overly subjective Leonard). Dealing with a situation that is *fait accompli*, Miss Bowen places the responsibility for chaos upon the middle class, represented by the Kelway family. Her treatment of the Rodneys is dualistic; Stella must share in the blame for war because she largely abdicated the responsibilities of her class; but Roderick, in planning to modernize the large estate he inherits in Ireland, carries hope into the future. And Louie, too, with her new baby and her own form of courage and integrity, is to be a source of strength in the new order.

The one piece of literature, however, which permeates the book is *Hamlet*. Miss Bowen could hardly have selected allusions to another work to underline more readily the heavy, black atmosphere which hangs over much of *The Heat of the Day*. There is much to remind one of the drama: Stella, long involved in self-debate; Harrison, on his first appearance, looming up from amid tomb-stones; parents guilty by virtue of selfishness; a mad woman speaking sense; a trip across water leading to action; Roderick ready, at the close, to take command. It is obvious there is something "rotten in the state," and there are allusions to the times being out of joint.

Several weeks pass before Stella confronts Robert with her infor-mation. Robert denies it. Shortly after, Harrison tells Stella he knows she has spoken to Robert; and he rather convincingly pinpoints the very night because Robert has altered the pattern of his behavior just as Harrison predicted he would when he became aware of being watched. In the penultimate chapter Robert admits the truth of Harrison's claim and seeks to justify his actions to Stella before he either slips or falls to his death from the roof of her apartment house. Previous to this admission of guilt, he has taken Stella to his home, Holme Delme; and, through her contact with his mother and his sister, Ernestine, she acquires a context for his final disclosures. The Holme Delme sequence contains the most castigating satire of the Bowen *oeuvre*.

Among Mrs. Kelway's antecedents are the father in Katherine Mansfield's "The Daughters of the Late Colonel," and, perhaps even more directly, the loathsome "Grannie" of D. H. Lawrence's *The Virgin and the Gypsy*. Such descriptive phrases as "diamond-like" and "ice-blue" have a particularly Lawrencean ring. Mrs. Kelway has dominated her home, has crushed her husband, and has sought to mold her children to her dehumanized sense of life. The sign at the entrance to the Holme Delme driveway is, "Caution Hidden Drive." Mr. Kelway, now dead, clearly was never taken seriously or permitted any self-expression; he was "only nominally allowed the fiction of being" the master.

Within her living room, Mrs. Kelway sits knitting (the fate of the nation?), and she is protected or withdrawn behind a series of screens. She is a version of the stereotyped Queen Victoria loftily stating "we are not amused." Stella quickly discovers the impossi-bility of conversation with her, for Mrs. Kelway is conscious only of what she herself says. Willful and inhuman, she is characterized by the imagery of the hunt and war: "decoy," "strategic," "command." To Stella, she is "wicked"; and what is most frightening is the indication that she is not unique but simply representative of a whole race of women. She is the solidification of a corrupt Puritan strain that is life denying and power conscious. The whole niggling, self-righteous, self-asserting approach to existence is captured in the great fuss over three pennies for Stella in order for her to mail a letter for Mrs. Kelway when she returns to London. Stella is appalled.

It is supremely ironic that this woman who spouts such comments as, "I have never thought of what I wanted," and "It is not a question of happiness," should be known as "Muttikins" (250). Suffering a self-conceived martyrdom, Mrs. Kelway is determined that hell shall be everyone's fate—and achieves her wish with the war. Robert, dispirited at his deepest level, says, "I was born wounded; my father's son" (263). In his room, Stella finds the walls lined with dozens of photographs of Robert at all ages and in all of the appropriate poses: with the great black dog, smiling in white flannels, standing next to a bright, attractive young woman, and so forth. He has not created a life; he has simply stepped into the pre-arranged poses. Robert tells Stella, "Each time I come back again into it I'm hit in the face by the feeling that I don't exist. . ." (112). The only communication in his home is in a "dead language" which gives rise to "repression, doubts, fears, subterfuges, and fibs" (247)

A fine touch is the fact that Mrs. Kelway and her daughter provide wartime sanctuary for two children. Mrs. Kelway likes to remind her son that she has taken the children "when it was not convenient . . ." (241). The situation is forcefully poignant viewed through the eyes of the girl Anne: "Never a heartbeat; never the light disregarding act, the random word or spontaneous kiss; never laughter . . . anger always in a smoulder. . . . Though she did not know it, she had never seen anyone being happy . . . " (254).

Robert has achieved a profound insight into the force of the middle-class power: "What else but an illusion could have such power?" (116). It is the nature of reality to reveal flaws, sooner or later; but these can be circumvented by the make-believe of self-importance and appropriateness. Lies, because they are total abstractions, are always true. But, whatever he has become, Robert has escaped being another Ernestine (the importance of being Ernestine?), who is "rather like a dog," who enjoys greater pleasure with a dog than with another human being, and whose face contains an "absense of human awareness" that is to Stella "quite startling" (102).

By revolting, Robert has avoided her fate, but the great danger in reaction is always overreaction. Miss Bowen characterizes Robert's siding with dictatorial powers as "romanticism fired once too often" (268). The final straw for Robert, so far as his society is concerned, was Dunkirk, where he was wounded. Apparently, he had gone to war seeing it as a sign of new hope; but after watching the "army of freedom queuing up to be taken off by pleasure boats," he was finished with England (263). One of the book's sad paradoxes is that his assertion of individuality rewarded him with a rich love affair which this very assertion foredoomed.

Miss Bowen is careful to present Robert as a revolutionary rather than as a Nazi sympathizer; for, if he is anti-England, he is not pro-German. The reader, along with Stella, sees Robert before his death not so much as a traitor but as a corrupt human who seized upon an unfortunate doctrine. He is a man who has chosen to rise above or to ignore nationalism: "there are no more countries left," he says, though he is telling Stella she is his country (258). What he seeks is change and the elimination of "the muddled, mediocre, damned" (259). As with the card-carrying, fellow travelers pursued by McCarthyism, Robert has given up on democracy where people are "kidded along from cradel to grave" (259). The Nazis are, for him, in the position most likely to accomplish the ends he desires; they are destroyers, if not builders. Muddle has left him desiring the clear and simple, and in Nazism he sees order. Stella can sympathize up to a point with Robert, but she can see that he has a greatly oversimplified world view and that he has lost sight of humanity in his own negative drive. There is reason to believe Miss Bowen sees Hitler as simply a manifestation of the Kelway way of life, and she believes that he rose to power on the backs of Germany's counterparts to the Kelways. At one point she characterizes the twists and turns of life in the upstairs of Holme Delme as "swastika-arms" (249). And there are also suggestions that Harrison's work is not unlike that of the Gestapo, implying that both combatants are alike. Thus, the novel is disclosing not simply the nature of England but the troubles underlying all of Europe or the Western world.

To turn to Harrison is not, suprisingly, to move away from Robert.

Near the end of the novel, Harrison tells Stella his Christian name is Robert. Robert and Harrison are thus mirror images—the one postulates the other. If the one has had too much home, the other has had too little. If Robert has yielded too much of himself to the private will, Harrison has dehumanized himself through submission to the public will. Throughout, Miss Bowen has hinted at the links between the men. Before he leaves her flat to die, Robert hears Stella explain that Harrison has him "at heart" (274). Only Robert justifies and provides Harrison with an identity. Privately, Harrison admits liking the war because it gives him a stature he otherwise lacks.

Little of Harrison's past is disclosed; but this lack indicates the point: he is rootless man. Stella appeals to him not as a source of passion but as a gracious woman with the ability to create a warm home; he seems happier with her flat than with her, and he is never more pleased than when she asks him to bring her a glass of milk from the kitchen. Indeed, he rather pathetically tells her that, for him, her flat is home. Since Robert can give Stella his heart but not his mind, it follows that Harrison's attachment to Stella is essentially in his mind; he cannot give her his heart, for, indeed, he may not have one to give. After Robert's death, he comes to visit Stella in her new flat. She rejects him, and he accepts this rejection "with relief" (311).

By this time, Stella has succumbed to exhaustion, all feeling spent. As she and Harrison sit talking, while an air raid is in progress, she tells him she may marry. When he tells her she owes it to her future husband to seek shelter, she denies it matters—love or death, she will take her chances. She accepts her role as a child of her times, and she knows she shares in the corruption of her generation. When, years ago, her husband, ironically named Victor, had returned wounded from World War I, he shocked her by claiming she did not love him and had departed to live with the nurse who had cared for him. He no sooner had gained a divorce than he had died.

At that time, her whole sorry travail of dislocation and doomed love had begun. Victor's family believes that Stella had provoked the divorce; and she has said nothing to deny it, preferring, as she tells Harrison, to appear a monster rather than a fool. Roderick, reared believing this of his mother, had learned the truth from Cousin Nettie, and had confronted his mother with it. Admitting the truth, she had asserted that its revelation came too late: "Whatever has been buried, surely, corrupts . . . " (220). She admits to Harrison, finally, that "there's an underside to me that I've hated, that you almost make me like . . . " (219). In the simplest terms, then, the main story of *The Heat of the Day* is the failure on a grand scale of feeling.

This being so, it is proper to discover in the characters Roderick and Louie a new purity and honesty of feeling. Roderick surprises his mother with his interest in his ailing Cousin Nettie and in hopes and plans he makes for his land in Ireland. The brief Irish passage appears as a momentary picture of sanity in an otherwise blighted world; and it is there that word of Montgomery's victory comes. Roderick, apparently, will find his roots in the remote rather than the recent past; and, in so doing, he will attach himself to a tradition of stability.

Louie, for her part, suggests the human capacity to endure, to withstand confusion, distortion, and disaster without losing her desire for basic domestic values. Left a war widow with a baby son, she is determined he will have a happy home; and her hard-won achievement of wisdom seems to assure it. Hers is the final vision of the future, the enduring grace and beauty of the three swans.

II A World of Love

After her wartime fiction and *The Demon Lover* (1945) story collection in particular, Miss Bowen could hardly have been expected to return untouched by the increased sense of psychic aberration the blitz and the buzz bombs gave to her more normal concerns—to such typical themes as hurt feelings and young love in a family situation—as she does in *A World of Love*. The connection between this novel and *The Heat of the Day* is rather explicit since Miss Bowen's opening sentence represents something of an in-joke, "The sun rose on a landscape still pale with the heat of the day before" (9). Though this novel is an experiment which did not succeed, for reasons to be noted and is, consequently, one of her least satisfactory books, it is interesting for several reasons. Among the foremost of these is its similarity to her earliest novels, *The Hotel* and *The Last September*. Like them, it has a beautiful girl in a relatively confined world whose instinctual quest for womanhood transmits shock waves which generally enlarge to the circumference of her sphere; but these narrative basics become transmuted into a fascinating variation through both the configurative and the

verbal creations of the author's increasingly metaphysical approach.
In *A World of Love*, Jane Danby, twenty, with "a face perfectly
ready to be a woman's, but not yet so," and her sister Maud, twelve,
whose "unmistakable content was moral force," become the instru-
ments which harrow their home (11; 171). Jane has just returned
from completing an English education paid for by her Aunt Antonia,
who has accompanied her home on one of her frequent sojourns.
Home is Montefort, owned by Antonia, a small, Irish country
manor; and it is presided over by Lilia Danby and farmed by her
husband Fred, Antonia's illegitimate cousin.

Not unexpectedly, the book opens with Montefort in a moribund
state. It is "half-sleep," and "The door no longer knew hospital-
ity . . . " (9). Conditions have actually been thus for twenty years,
and at the root of the trouble is the former owner, Guy. Details from
the past which account for the unsatisfactory lives and relationships
of the elder Danbys are released throughout the novel. Antonia,
her cousin Guy, and Fred, the "by-blow," have grown up at
Montefort. Gifted with trememdous vitality, Antonia and Guy have
lived something of a Wuthering Heights existence. Fred recalls,
"You and he were something out of the common. . . . The way you
two were, you could have run the world" (120).

By the time World War I began and Guy had joined the army,
Antonia had fallen in love with him; but, during the course of one
of his leaves, he had become engaged to an English girl, Lilia, then
seventeen. By the time Guy had departed for the last time to France
in 1918, he had acquired another woman, a fact known by both
Antonia and Lilia, who have yet to meet. Not until the end of the
novel do the two women bring this information into the open. As the
narrator eventually observes, Guy "had stirred up too much; he had
scattered round him more promises as to some dreamed-of extreme
of being than one man could have hoped to live to honour" (145).

After Guy's death in battle, Antonia inherits Montefort and
decides to do something for Lilia. This decision, in retrospect,
appears unfortunate, for "never had intervention proved more
fatal" (18); the narrator suggests that Lilia would have been better
left alone. At any rate, when, after ten years, Lilia remains unwed,
Antoina feels justified in taking matters into her own hands. She
tells Fred, who has been drifting about, that she will turn Montefort
over to him for a share in the profits if he will marry Lilia. An
obvious admirer of Guy, Fred agrees that "Guy's girl" is worth

a look. The wedding takes place, though not until Antonia has threatened Lilia with the withdrawal of additional assistance if she refuses.

When Jane is seven, her mother bolts for London and announces she will not return. Once more Antonia threatens her; and, after softening her, Antonia dispatches Fred to bring her home. Fred's wooing succeeds, they return, and the reunion is marked by the conception of Maud. Since all of these events precede the story proper, it should be evident that *A World of Love* is burdened with more exposition than any other Bowen novel. However, while all of this information helps explain why Montefort is not a happy home, it does not really account for the psychic state of the adults. These states are implied as the present action—the reactive action that Montefort is more than due for—unfolds.

While Jane is rummaging around in the attic, she finds, or, as the narrator views it, a bundle of love letters finds her. The letters were written by Guy while he was at Montefort to an unknown person. A ready recipient for romance, Jane becomes enamored of them. When Guy writes, "I wish you were," Jane can cry, "I am!" Not unexpectedly the letters have considerable impact on the whole house, revivifying thoughts of Guy especially for Antonia and Lilia. The letters create tensions for three emotionally intense days (the countryside, meanwhile, is suffering prostrating heat) at the end of which they are burned by a wiser Jane, symbolically releasing the omnipresent Guy; and conditions at Montefort have altered obviously for the better.

What gradually emerges is the extent of Guy's impact upon these people. Having been dazzled by his tremendous energy, they have never truly comprehended his death, which explains why the narrator sees him as a presence rather than as a ghost. It might be assumed he has remained as a force in their memories, but this is not the case: "not memories was it but expectations which haunted Montefort. His immortality was in their longings, while each year mocked the vanishing garden" (145). Guy's contemporaries are never unaware that "The living [are] living in his life-time. . . . They were incomplete" (65). Living in these terms consists in enduring a timeless limbo.

Perhaps Lilia's waiting is the most strained of all, for her whole existence as Guy's intended ("if not the Beloved, what was Lilia?") is frozen in a state of suspension. Like Stella in *The Heat of the*

Day, Lilia has lived a lie—as if she preferred, like Stella, to be a monster rather than a fool in her own eyes, although this cognition implies more self-awareness on her part than the text allows. It is more accurate to say she has never really permitted herself to confront the truth; for, once a true reassessment of Guy begins to take place, she can admit to herself that "not till today had she wholly taken account. Guy was dead, and only today at dinner had she sorrowed for him" (72).

For her part, Antonia has acted as if it were necessary to keep everything going, to keep Guy's world intact until his return. Her relationship with Lilia appears as almost the only noteworthy event of her life, or of their lives: "Thrown together, they had adhered: virtually, nothing more than this had happened to them since their two girlhoods" (74). Much of her time literally consists of putting in time, sleeping late, drinking alone, napping, lying on the beach. Antonia's sharpness and bossiness are those of a person bored and expecting to stay so (interestingly, she calls the vital Jane "a bore").

Fred, the man caught in the middle, is aware that he is Guy's substitute and that, as such, he has hardly been fairly regarded for himself. He, of course, knows nothing of yet another woman. Of the three, he is the only one who has sought to remain somewhat vital— if the rumors of Irish lasses down the lane are true. Denied the proper role of man of the family, as Maud takes occasion to indicate to Antonia, he has channeled himself into hard work.

Jane, Lilia, and Antonia all experience the same doubts when they begin to emerge from their respective states of illusion; they cannot be certain of their immediate direction. Lilia thinks, "What had now happened must either kill her or, still worse, force her to live . . ." (72). The ludicrous situation of seeing the beautiful Jane having her first love affair with a packet of letters brings both Lilia and Jane up short. Officially, the fiction that the letters rightfully belong to Lilia persists to the close; but she and Antonia know otherwise and, in the end, so too does Jane. Lilia's first active response to the sense of change in the air is to have her hair cut in the recent style, which represents a return to an earlier day when bobbing and shingling were fashionable.

But this symbolic attempt to retrieve time results in an unexpected confrontation. While Lilia is sitting alone in the Montefort garden, she suddenly senses the approach of someone—she is certain that it is Guy—when in walks Fred. He, it appears, was and is her destiny.

He has brought her the letters, which he has taken from Maud who had taken them from under the rock where they had been hidden (abandoned?) by Jane, in the belief that they are hers. Lilia is touched by his act, and the next thing Montefort witnesses is their driving off together for a spin in the old Danby Ford. When Lilia later admits to Antonia that she knew of Guy's other woman, her settlement with the past is complete; and her emergence as a "new woman" seems assured.

It is Maud who starts Jane on her road to awareness and who provides the finishing touches to Antonia's emergence as a more sympathetic being. Traversing the thigh-deep bracken along the river, enfolded in a romantic mood, Jane is suddenly accosted by Maud, who yells, first, "What are *you* playing?" and, then, "What are you pretending about that tree?" (70-71). These questions are sufficient to make Jane feel foolish and recognize the silliness of her affair with Guy. She is now ready for a second test, and this comes in the form of a real letter from the nouveau riche English woman who has recently purchased the local castle. Vesta Latterly, having earlier spotted Jane and thinking the girl's beauty would be an adornment at her table, invites her to a dinner party. While *A World of Love* largely concerns itself with the dangers of past events, it also presents a counterstatement about the poise and sense of responsibility a past can bestow—a lesson Jane learns at the castle. And a lesson she needs to learn, since, daughter of Montefort, she has "an instinctive aversion from the past . . . a sort of pompous imposture . . . " (48).

The Latterly world proves phantasmagoric. Vesta's circle is comprised of hulks who have surrendered their soul to Mamon— as Jane recognizes. An older Irishman comparing the past and present tells her, "These days, one goes where the money is—with all due respect to this charming lady. Those days, we went where the people were" (94). Jane knows Guy often frequented the castle; and, when there is an empty place at the table, she imagines him present, not now as her lover, but as her ancestor from a nobler time. Though tipsy with her first martini, she can see that Guy is more real than those present; for, as old Terrance has told her, "You can't buy the past" (93). Jane's acceptance of Montefort and its heritage is akin to Lois Farquar's discovery of the reality of Danielstown in *The Last September*.

Rather ironically, through the dissolute Vesta Jane meets the man who may prove to be a real lover. Unable to meet the son of an acquaintance who is flying in from Colorado, Vesta sends Jane with her chauffeur to Shannon to meet him. He proves a tall, handsome young man; and, as they confront each other, "They no sooner looked but they loved" (224). Out of context, this sudden love may appear as unduly sentimental, even for a highly poetic novel. Coming as it does, however, in a novel troubled by subjectivism, it serves as a judgment on the willingness of one who has demonstrated her capacity to distinguish reality and fantasy to avail herself of the creative "chance" of life.

Antonia's initial response to Guy's resurrection through the letters verges on the pantheistic. She feels the old force of Guy upon her emanating from the darkness of the night: "She was met at once like a wind-like rushing towards her out of the dark—her youth and Guy's from every direction. . . . All round Montefort there was going forward an entering back again into possession: the two, now one again, were again here . . . " (113). Antonia feels as if "Doom was lifted from her" and that "time again was into the clutch of herself and Guy" (113-14). Her near mystical experience is like the final intensity of light, the orgasmic sputter, before the bulb dims.

But, in the dawn of the day after, Antonia is confronted by too much evidence that the static Montefort world she has expended her energy and effort to sustain is breaking up; and that, far from living in a timeless world, the years have taken their toll of her. Lilia and Fred seem bound now to have at this late date, if not love, a relationship which is truly their own. Lilia's admission of Guy's other woman and her refusal to accept the packet of letters in effect earn her release from the past. Jane's entry into the Latterly world, if only as a passing observer, informs Antonia that the girl is moving beyond her grasp and into a life of her own. Angered over Jane's first contact with the castle, Antonia is mild and interested as Jane departs into Vesta's sphere again at the close.

It is Maud, however, who administers, unintentionally, the final blows to Antonia's hardened mold. Like an emerging spirit, she comes spouting forth "maledictions" from the Psalms. When Maud expresses her views about her father's role, or about what his role should be in the family, Antonia must confess, "Maud as a character had to be re-assessed . . ." (166). Antonia, like Jane before her, is forced to assess her conduct from the cold light of Maud's viewpoint; and the experience is discomfiting: Antonia flees her own bedroom, leaving "the field to Maud" (171). Maud's final impact results from her devotion to Big Ben whose confirmation of nine o'clock on the radio she eagerly awaits each evening. Sitting in the dining room hearing "passionless Big Ben," Antonia flinches before "The sound of time, inexorably coming as it did, at once . . . absolute and fatal" (193). At the same time Jane, studying her aunt, thinks: "And I shall never see Antonia again. . . . Something has happened. Somehow she's gone,—She's old" (194).

Throughout, the narrator indirectly comments on Guy through Maud's imaginary companion, Gay David. Quite like the living members of her family, Gay is subjected to rough handling from Maud. And, if Guy's contemporaries have given him debilitating obeisance, Gay receives an unceasing flow of punches and kicks. Maud's most obvious predecessor in the novels is Theodora Thirdman of *Friends and Relations*. The narrator, along with Antonia, may well ask of Maud, "what might the future not have to fear from her?" But, in a world where the temptation to effortless ennui is so great, such people are shown to be valuable.

If by the term "poetic novel," a phrase frequently attached to *A World of Love*, is meant a work with a high degree of implication, or that is highly impressionistic, then the novel is aptly generalized. This novel is Miss Bowen's most extreme one in this regard, and it must also be regarded as one of her least popular and least appealing books. The poetic novel may simply be an anomaly unlikely to appeal to many.

One problem with books which carry a style disproportionately elaborate to their content is that, once the technique has been fathomed, little else remains. Or again we can feel that impressionism has been employed as an easy short-cut. The story demands that Jane alter, and, presto, the change takes place. The sense that an author is seeking to gain approbation by admitting the nature of her work and by attempting to make the reader a coconspirator is likely to be offensive. The Latterly world, for example, simply a straw-man cartoon, prompts Jane to call its habitues "a pack of cards." There is everywhere a verbal elaboration that too frequently exists as an end in itself—as, for example, in the description informing us of an airplane landing in the rain:

And the sky, as though reminded of something else, began at this moment to let fall far-apart tepid drops; each so surprising, as it splashed on to cuff, forehead or eyelid, as to seem larger than it was; each too individual and momentous to be rain. The drops, one could imagine, could be heard; and they distracted attention from any diluted humming above the cloud-ceiling; or did so till this began to concentrate into a pinpoint and pierce through. The sound went on, like pressure upon a nerve, and the plane came sifting through into visibility; one watched its hesitating descent to such, alas, a remote part of the airport that, landing, it dropped again out of view. It remedied this by coming taxiing endlessly, endlessly inward along the runways, first at one angle, then at another, and so absurd was its progress in this manner, one could have wept. (222-23)

This passage is simply not work worthy of extended attention.

III   The Little Girls

The Little Girls is Miss Bowen's most intricate and subtle novel: intricate in the relationship of its components and subtle in its psychology. Allusiveness is carried to a tantalizing edge where one more step would plunge everything into an incomprehensible state. Yet the surface amost belies this allusiveness; the author has never sustained sprightlier pacing or more rapid dialogue. This engaging surface and a clever unfolding of character psychology save this novel from the fate of *A World of Love*. Though lacking in the power of her best work, *The Little Girls* is among the most impressive of Miss Bowen's novels.

Initially asking what the consequences might be if a person reopened relationships which have been dormant for fifty years, the novel provides one highly imaginative answer. Dinah Delacroix, still an attractive, active woman at sixty-one, decides to contact the two women with whom she was most intimate when they were all eleven and in their last term together at Saint Agatha's in the summer of 1914. By the end of Part I, Dinah (known as Dicey), has entertained at her country home Clare Burkin-Jones (Mumbo), divorcee and successful business woman, and Sheila Artworth (Sheikie), wife of a man whose family has long been prominent in Southstone, home of the now vanished Saint Agatha's.

Part II moves back in time to deal with the closing weeks spent together by the threesome at school. The central activity follows the girls' decision to bury secretly in the school garden a coffer containing a note written in blood in a private code and various objects including a contribution by each girl known only to herself. Not until late in the novel is the nature of these contributions revealed. The section culminates with a term-end picnic and farewells, which endure until Dinah's notices in the personal columns of the *Times* and other English papers effect the reunion.

The action of Part III follows from that of the opening sequence; Dinah talks her reluctant partners into digging up the coffer even though, as Sheila is in a position to point out, it now lies in the garden of a private home. The coffer is found empty, a discovery upsetting to Dinah. And more surprising is the collapse Dinah suffers two weeks later after being scolded by sturdy, no-nonsense Clare. The closing portion of the book revolves about the bed in which Dinah is prostrate. Sheila is on hand and in command of Dinah's two married sons; her handsome widower neighbor, Major Frank Wilkins; and her youthful Maltese houseboy, Francis; and the now hangdog and troubled Clare.

Even this bare outline should reveal how the novel appears to shift in intent at the opening of the coffer. Seeming concern for the retrieval of both chest and friendship is displaced by the psychological mystery of Dinah's behavior and, retroactively, by the motivation underlying the apparent spontaneity of her decision to contact the past. The shift is, of course, seeming rather than real. Basically, the book is constructed on a cunning switch. Of the three women, Dinah appears to be the only one living a satisfying life. Why Clare and Sheila are reluctant to expose themselves to a woman whose advertisements bespeak an adventuresomeness they no longer possess is understandable. Yet events lead to a reversal in which Dinah emerges as the most troubled of the trio. Only gradually do we come to fathom, as Clare most evidently does, Dinah's problem and to comprehend what she means when she puzzles the others by saying such things as, "Can't you see what's happened? This us three. This going back, I mean. This began as a game, *began* as a game. Now—you see?—it's got me!" (188). The reader can take some consolation initially that neither Clare nor Sheila "sees" either.

Dinah, it becomes apparent, has had an easy life; and she has become, as Clare points out to her, "in many ways very wonderful." But, in summoning her old friends, she has encountered fears and doubts about the reality of her existence and the quality of its feeling. Though it is not crucial, it is not clear whether Dinah's doubts rose before the re-encounter or following it. Dinah says, though after the fact, that she recalled her friends for hundreds of reasons (all of the facts of her life?); but Clare believes Dinah "chanced, not chose, to want Sheila and herself again" (276).

Quite appropriately, Dinah's crisis invokes for her memories of *Macbeth* and unstated echoes of life's "signifying nothing." The whole affair of the coffer suddenly becomes a symbolic testing ground for her. When illumination finally comes to Clare, she says, over the slumbering body of Dinah, "There being nothing was what you were frightened of all the time, eh? Yes. Yes, it was terrible looking down into that empty box" (277). And Frank reported earlier that, when he and Francis had lifted the distraught woman into bed, she had cried, "It's all gone, was it ever there? No, never there. Nothing. No, no, no . . ." (258). Again it is not really clear whether Dinah is referring to her own life or to life in general; but from her point of view, the distinction hardly matters.

The first indication that Dinah is cracking occurs when the women return for drinks after their digging expedition to Artworths. Having hardly arrived, Dinah announces that she must leave. When Sheila tells her that her home "won't run away," Dinah answers, "That's what it *has* done. . . . Everything has. *Now* it has, you see. Nothing's real any more . . . " (188). We may recollect with interest that, upon her introduction, Dinah is characterized as "a woman, intent on what she was doing to the point of trance . . . " (3). If, in the first stage of her awakening, Dinah must question the nature of her own reality, in the second stage, her personal being is called to an accounting. Taking umbrage at one of Dinah's remarks, Clare gives her an objective characterization of herself; she calls Dinah "Circe," and "a cheat. A player-about. Never once have you played fair, all along the line"; and then she adds, "Some of us more than *think* we feel" (230).

This announcement amplifies earlier statements Clare and Sheila have made about Dinah. When Dinah's notices first came to their attention, and Clare and Sheila met to decide whether or not to answer her, they most readily recall Dinah as "too self-centered" (40). During the book, they refer to her as "Young Lochinvar" and "Ba-lamb." And, after seeing the present-day Dinah, Sheila can still say she has "never yet outgrown being a selfish child" (201). When she becomes quite worked up over Dinah, she says, "What makes me so mad is the way things are showered on to her that she hasn't the sense to value or understand. Showered" (201). More-over, the whole world built about Dinah attests to its unreality and its accommodation of her. Francis, with his Walter Mittylike projec-

tions of secret-service adventure, is a fitting occupant of a demi-
paradise in which his mistress has at her beck and call a handsome
gentleman who helps her with gardening in a garden where innocence clearly prevails. The grotto with its fanciful collection of
momentos pried loose from people, though they are items "which
they couldn't have normally borne to part with," and a place destined to confound future people is the perfect activity for an
individual who enjoys, even if she does not comprehend, life.

In addition to the other names she calls Dinah, Clare claims she
is an "enchantress's child," and this term provides a clue for a
reading of the wonderfully realized 1914 scenes. Dinah and her
mother, Mrs. Piggott (pig it?),[2] live in the cozy little cottage Feverel
Cottage (can we doubt the author's intent that we remember the
raising of Richard in George Meredith's *The Ordeal of Richard
Feverel*?). Here, supported by a wealthy cousin, Mrs. Piggott
indulges her two loves, fine china and books (later there is repeated
reference to the books in Dinah's bedroom); here, "Mrs. Piggott
and [Dinah] had . . . spun round themselves a tangible web, through
whose transparency, layers deep, one glimpsed some fixed, perhaps
haunted, other dimension" (85).

Though there are passing references to the visits of Major Birkin-
Jones to Feverel Cottage, it is not until the end of Part II that it is
possible to comprehend his love for Dinah's mother. On the verge
of reporting for active duty, for war is imminent, he appears at the
picnic late to say farewell to Mrs. Piggott. She has been willing to
take, if not to give; when she folds her arms and presses "them
against herself," he says, "You're cold" (151). Later it is disclosed
that Dinah's father threw himself under a train before her birth;
and, although no explanation for his action is proffered, none seems
needed. When Mrs. Piggott is sick in bed, Dinah wishes to quote a
line from *Macbeth* and chooses, suggestively, "Was my father a
traitor, mother?" (244). This question implies her recognition of
what the loss of a father may have cost her life.

Technically, the novel's middle section is a tour de force in maintaining our attention on the surface action and implanting hints
about Major Birkin-Jones in such a way that the disclosure of his
love comes at once as surprise to us—and all the more so for having
taken place under our very eyes.

Dinah's illness proves double-edged. For her, it serves as
purgative; for her circle of acquaintances, it serves as rejuvenation.

Frank is stunned. A selfish man himself, as Sheila observes, it is ironical that he is not aware that Dinah has fobbed him off, literally and figuratively, with a mask. But he does come to bury his head in her pillow. Sheila, hitherto somewhat ineffectual, finds a true outlet for her desire to be useful. Tending Dinah gives her an opportunity to repay her one-time exit from the deathroom of her lover which has haunted her; and, by way of reward, she inherits, as it were in Dinah's offspring, the sons she has longed to have. For her part, Clare realizes how she has permitted business to dehumanize her and deny the feelings of others; for, standing over the prostrate Dinah, she says to herself: "I did not comfort you. Never have I comforted you. Forgive me" (277).

Clare's final admission of responsibility toward others is analogous with the change Dinah also experiences. Fittingly, the book ends with Dinah waking from a long sleep. The brief exchange between herself and Clare reveals, for all its terseness, that Dinah has shed her childlike attitude to life along with her terrifying sense of meaninglessness, and assumed her proper role in the present. Upon awakening, Dinah queries: "Who's there?" "Mumbo." "Not Mumbo. Clare. Clare, where have you been?" (277). It is a paradox worthy of life that the innocence which came to trouble Dinah is the kind which made possible not only her own salvation but also the resurrection of her closest friends. This paradox recurs consistently in the Bowen novels.

When we at last learn what items the girls placed in the coffer, it can be seen that each buried something really requisite to her life. If not in actuality, then metaphysically, events allow the women to repossess what was secretly hidden. Dinah's contribution was a gun, symbol of violence, without which, according to other Bowen novels, life is incomplete. The results of violence, if not the act itself, appear in the novel in the form of the bruise on Dinah's forehead, discovered when she is found by Francis slumped over. And, along with the late disclosure of Mr. Piggott's violent death, come several hints of contemplated suicide on Dinah's part.

Clare buried a copy of Shelley's poetry, believing herself through with it. Her failed marriage and her protective brittleness readily enough indicate her loss of a sense of poetry in life and her indifference to the humanitarianism Shelley advocated. Not so readily translatable as the gun and the book is the sixth toe which Sheila contributed to the casket. But, when she mentions how embarrassed she was over the toe, it may be surmised that, in being unwilling to accept her fate or situation, her unwillingness to acknowledge the sliver of flesh has remained as her inability to accept the events of her life, one which accounts for her tensions and hypersensitivity.

IV   Eva Trout

A World of Love and *The Little Girls* seek to justify the image of hope and promise which survive the holocast of *The Heat of the Day*. Both novels find rehabilitation possible in the modern world, but Miss Bowen's tenth novel, *Eva Trout or Changing Scenes*, discloses that the scene has indeed changed; the honeymoon is over. The world of *Eva Trout* is askew and romantically bloated; it is studded with heavy operatic names like Iseult, Eric, and Constantine. Fittingly, for a heroine with the sturdy, fundamental name of Eva Trout, Eva desires normalcy; but she, as the novel implies, is asking too much of our times. Long denied a sane, stable existence, Eva, on the verge of reaping her desires and of achieving respectable communication with the world, is struck down in a melodramatically bizarre and ludicrously contrived manner. *Eva Trout* is Miss Bowen's contribution to the "black humor" of the 1960's. What makes this report tolerable is, typically enough with Miss Bowen, the romping delight of the narrative voice which delights in the inexhaustibleness of the human condition, whatever its manifestations.

Mrs. Iseult Arbles, on her way to visit Eva, pauses in Broadstairs to visit the Charles Dickens's room in Bleak House. This room gives the narrator an opportunity to observe, "It took Dickens not to be eclipsed by Eva" (133). Eva, a "she-Cossack," is the largest of the author's heroines, both literally and figuratively. But she shares with her predecessors an abnormal rearing which renders her conduct of relationships highly unnatural. A combination of miseducation or noneducation has made Eva a conversational misfit; as a result, drama follows from her encounters with communication. When is Eva to be believed, and to what extent? Conversely, how will she interpret or misinterpret the signals she receives from the abnormal or nervous human beings surrounding her? A trout out of water in a neurotic world, Eva wants a husband and a child. But how to acquire them?

The book begins when Eva is boarding with Eric and Iseult Arbles who live on a fruit farm in Worcestershire. She is almost twenty-

four; and, when she has her birthday, she is to come into a fortune.
Chiefly she occupies herself with the local rectory children of Mr.
and Mrs. Dancey. Her favorite is Henry, twelve, perhaps because
"she [can] not boss him and he [can] mortify her . . ." (15). Quite
evidently Eva is bored with her situation; and, like Bowen heroines
before her, she is eager to begin her own life. The principal action
of "Part I" involves Eva's sudden and secretive departure for the
Broadstairs area where she purchases a large furnished home near
the sea. Life, presumably, begins with a home, preferably an older
one which boasts a past bespeaking settlement. When she becomes
wealthy, Eva fills this home with the latest in electrical equipment.
The electric typewriter, stereo, movie projector, tape recorder, and
computer (on order) are to place her abreast of her time and, perhaps, represent a reflexive determination to modernize her capacity
to communicate.

After the house is to come what is more readily purchasable by
Eva than a husband—a child. But Eva's nature does not permit her
simply to fly to the United States where she intends to make this
transaction; she must prepare the way. During her visit with Eva,
Iseult proposes that Eva spend Christmas with the Arbles. Eva
refuses on the grounds that she will, at that time, be having a baby.
Unhindered by Eva, Iseult, realizing a time lapse of nine months
between an earlier visit to Eva by Eric at Christmas, assumes the
obvious.

Eva's announcement is her way of settling an old grudge against
Iseult which dates from the days when Iseult was Miss Smith,
teacher in a private girls' school, and Eva was one of her pupils.
Eva arrived at the school after she had wearied of trailing about the
world with her father and his male lover, Constantine, and had
insisted that she be allowed to settle into a more natural life. Having
passed through the hands of a series of indifferent governesses who
served in place of her mother long since killed in a plane crash, Eva
is elated to be recognized as existing by Miss Smith; and she experiences the first passion of her life: "Till Iseult came, no human being
had ever turned upon Eva their full attention—an attention which
could seem to be love. Eva knew nothing of love but that it existed—
that, she should know, having looked on at it. *Her* existence had gone
by under a shadow: the shadow of Willy Trout's total attachment
to Constantine" (18). Like other Bowen characters who are charged
with reciprocating the idealistic demands of other Bowen heroines,

Iseult hedges in her response and Eva construes her caution as rejection. So the seed of antipathy comes to be planted.

When, a few years later, Willy Trout commits suicide and Constantine assumes the role of guardian, Eva decides she would like to board with the intellectual Iseult and her working-man husband on their fruit farm. The Arbles welcome Eva—but for financial reasons. Like Portia in *The Death of the Heart*, Eva enters a household where marriage is proving less than satisfactory: "the marriage was founded on a cerebral young woman's first physical passion" (19). Eric is disappointed because there are no children; Iseult, already chaffing at a restrictive life with a failed fruit farmer cum garage man, is troubled by his declining interest in her. Eric's eventual interest in Eva is not calculated to ease matters at all. Eva's pregnancy gambit proves to be the coup de grâce to the marriage.

Not until eight years later does Eva learn that the Arble marriage failed to survive her implied relationship with Eric. However, this novel, and others by the author, shares an ambivalence toward violence wrought by the subjective innocent. There is no hint of loss, no sense of real pain over the Arbles' separation. Upon her return to England, Eva begins to pick up the ends of her earlier life. She finds Eric living contentedly with a common-law wife who has born him two children. Iseult is located on the Continent but is easily enough lured back into Eva's orbit. Before long Iseult and Eric are back together again, and this time, seemingly, they are truly in love. No mention is made of the two children and their mother. Such is the modern world.

The baby boy Eva acquires surreptitiously in Chicago and christens Jeremy proves to be a deaf-mute; and, in the years of Eva's absence from England, she has lived in a series of American cities in an effort to find help for her son. When he is eight, she decides the time has come for them to return to her country and to locate, though such is never stated directly, a father for Jeremy. They settle in a London hotel; and, after Jeremy is set to sculpting with a private tutor, Eva leaves for Cambridge to seek Henry Dancey who is now a student.

The final sequence of absurdity has its beginning when Iseult, back from London, "borrows" Jeremy from his sculpting instructress in order to have a visit with him since she still assumes he has been fathered by Eric. When Jeremy fails to return to his mother at the hotel, she becomes distraught; her mind leaps immediately to the probability of kidnapping. Before she does anything drastic, however, Jeremy wanders in. He, of course, cannot explain matters to her. Unnerved, Eva decides to quit London for a time; and, leaving all of their possessions at the hotel, she and Jeremy make for Fontainebleau. While here, she fortuitously becomes acquainted with a doctor and his wife who have been working with deaf-mutes with considerable success. The couple agrees to accept Jeremy as long as he can live with them and Eva will absent herself. When Eva returns to England and Henry, she proposes marriage to the young man, who really is quite fond of her. He refuses. Then, as usual with Eva, who prefers to have the appearance of propriety if not the reality of it for the benefit of the Arbles and Constantine, she asks him to depart with her from Victoria Station as if he were going to marry her, and he agrees to her request.

Thus, the culminating scene takes place at Victoria. And indeed Iseult, Eric, and Constantine are on hand in a festive mood—as is Jeremy, who has been brought from France for the occasion. Before coming to the station, however, he has visited his old hotel to pick up some things left behind. He is delighted and surprised to find among the Trout goods a pistol, a real one, though he is not aware that it is. Miss Bowen has earlier shown how the gun became so located. It belongs to Eric but turned up among Iseult's possessions when she went to the Continent. She has decided to bring it back to England in order to return it to him. Not wishing to carry the gun about with her, she is inspired, when she becomes aware of Eva's stored possessions in London, to deposit the gun temporarily with these.

There are two moments of drama at Victoria. First, Henry tells Eva that he has changed his mind; he really wishes to marry her. Second, Jeremy, rushing forward to greet his mother, playfully points the gun at her, pulls the trigger, and the gun fires. Eva drops to the pavement dead, and the novel ends. Though the book invokes the Dickens world as a context for Eva, it more fittingly reminds one of Thomas Hardy and of *Jude the Obscure* in particular. Eva, like Jude, has aspirations which both her limited awareness and her incessant misfortune abrogate.

The novel is very entertaining; Miss Bowen is too much the professional for *Eva Trout* to be otherwise. But in retrospect, we wonder if it adds up to much. A residue of dissatisfaction seems almost inevitable. Miss Bowen's best work gives a sense of the untidiness and unpredictability of life. Her books realize her own insistence that major characters retain the capacity to unfold throughout a narrative. *Eva Trout*, conversely, is held too tightly in thrall by its basic narrative diagram. Eva, child of violence and seeker of a normal life, reverses the usual sequence of husband, child, house; and, when she is on the verge of attaining the husband, she comes full circle to her true inheritance of violence.

Eva is one of Miss Bowen's best ideas for a heroine but one of her weakest realizations. A credibility gap exists between the Eva that the other characters see and talk about and her character as actually evoked for the reader. Though there is an insistence on her oddity, the oddness consists largely of a rather predictable stupidity. Compared with such an advanced innocent as Emmeline of *To the North*, Eva emerges as a crude creation. Emmeline exists as an authentic public figure who is finally tripped up by the gradually disclosed flaw lurking in her psychological makeup. Too, Eva's world disarms her as a Dickensian figure. Constantine, the American professor, the Chicago characters, the rental agent, and the sculptress are all of a piece with her.

Critics of the book, while finding much in the performance to praise, arrive at the position we have expressed; but they have used the word "hollowness." Mary Ellmann writes, "after a long career in fiction, a lifetime of talent, Elizabeth Bowen has a particular right to propose now, if she likes, that the novel is all words— not portentous at all, but finely frivolous." [3] And Bernard Bergonzi concludes, "I could not fight back a sense of mounting incredulity about what I was being told . . . the author's desire to make tight aesthetic patterns out of life takes precedence over any inclination to convey the sense of life itself." [4]

CHAPTER 5

A Divine Comedy: The Short Stories

> There is a house that is no
> more a house
> Upon a farm that is no more a farm
> And in a town that is no more a town.

> —Robert Frost, "Directive"

Miss Bowen has published more than seventy short stories, but this number includes several brief anecdotal pieces. Many of these stories first appeared in such publications as the *Cornhill Magazine*, the *Listener*, and *The New Yorker*; and most of them are republished in one of her eight collections of short stories. Her first collections were *Ann Lee's and Other Stories* (1920) and *Encounters* (1923), which were republished in 1950 as *Early Stories*. These were followed by *Joining Charles* (1929), *The Cat Jumps* (1934), *Look at All Those Roses* (1941), and *The Demon Lover* (1952). Two later volumes in which the author made personal selections from among her stories were *Stories by Elizabeth Bowen* (1959) and *A Day in the Dark* (1965).

We do not confront such a body of work easily, for, as Edward Mitchell has commented, "Treating the representative majority of an author's short fiction is not the most congenial of critical undertakings. Such an endeavor invites organization by exclusion, or inclusion at the expense of organization."[1] However, Miss Bowen's stories appear to fall naturally enough into three main thematic groupings, and a discussion of her best eighteen or so stories gives a fair indication of her talent for diversification within her relatively narrow concerns.

In her Preface to *A Day in the Dark*, Miss Bowen explains her unconcern for chronology in arranging stories from a thirty-six-year span because she takes it "to be a myth" that a writer's development may be ascertained through successive stories. She maintains that "a writer of short stories is at his or her best sometimes, and sometimes not; and this is true equally of any age or in any year at which he or she happens to be writing." A survey of Miss Bowen's stories appears to substantiate her position so far as her own work is concerned, and it therefore justifies a nonchronological approach to her stories.

As might properly be expected, almost everything that has been said about the author's interests and techniques in her novels applies equally to her stories. A few generalizations are worth repeating, and there is one noteworthy difference. By and large, the protagonists are sensitive, educated, well-mannered females moving through a reasonably well-to-do world. The point of view is almost always omniscient, and most stories include generous portions of dialogue. All but a few contain incisive but impressionistic descriptive passages which help to establish and sustain mood and tone. Many of the stories show a greater freedom in their handling of time than the novels. The interplay between present and past time (not readily conveyed by analyses), along with elliptical conversation and terse narrative details, contributes to a "difficult" and challenging style. Not a writer given to concessions, Miss Bowen says: "I expect the reader to be as (reasonably) imaginative as myself." The stories employ what the author calls "a free form," which she describes as "impressionism lightly laced with psychology. . . ." There are times, especially in *The Demon Lover* collection, when we might wish to amend this statement to read, "heavily laced with psychology."

It is on the matter of psychology that Miss Bowen's stories differ most from her longer fiction. Her better short stories, on the whole, investigate psychological states (what the author calls "fantasy") which are more unusual than those portrayed in the novels. In the Preface to *Stories by Elizabeth Bowen*, the author explains why this is so:

Looking through this selection I have made, I find fantasy strongly represented. Critics may possibly say, too much so? Yet these, I still maintain, are my better stories. If I were a short-story writer only, I might well seem to be out of balance. But recall, more than half my life is under the steadying influence of the novel, with its calmer, stricter, more orthodox demands: into the novel goes such taste as I have for rational behaviour and social portraiture. The short story, as I see it to be, allows for what is crazy about humanity: obstinacies, inordinate heroisms, "immortal longings." At no time, even in the novel, do I consider realism to be my forte.

We have entitled this chapter "A Divine Comedy" because her principal story categories readily lend themselves to being characterized as Hell, Purgatory, and Heaven as each relates to Miss Bowen's pervasive concern with individual fulfillment. The Hell stories portray people entrapped in destructive or stagnating circumstances, capacities, or attitudes; the Purgatory inhabitants are those who, though likewise possessed of dehumanizing views or pursuing an unexamined life, are confronted with situations or characters which may "save" them; Heaven encompasses the most explicitly irrational individuals—those who are employing "divine" ways of maintaining their identity in the face of threatening circumstances.

I *Varieties of Hell*

In the modest story "Mrs. Windermere," a pleasant young woman, Esmée, having met an older Mrs. Windermere in Italy during a vacation, runs into her in London while shopping. The insensitive older woman, presuming upon their "friendship" and her age, takes possession of the unforceful, lady-like Esmée and subjects her to an endless luncheon which the latter endures rather than be rude. Esmée's experience is more humorous than harmful, but it contains in miniature the destructive circumstances her counterparts face in the usual Bowen stories of this type.

Understandably, these are Miss Bowen's harshest stories, for they constitute a vision of the wasteland while cataloguing various causes of entrapment. Sometimes the will of a strong but misdirected person imposes itself upon an innocent or helpless victim ("The Little Girl's Room"); often a character's own desires or ego twist life ("A Love Story"); at other times a person crumbles before forces he can hardly or only vaguely define ("The Disinherited"). Some characters are not even conscious of their entrapment; but, when they are, enlightenment has come only after the process is complete.

Compared with other stories, these generally originate in relatively normal circumstances, a fact which contributes to their chilling effect since we are reminded of the proximity of limbo. The chill is also reinforced by Miss Bowen's detached, stoical humor. Though the situations portrayed are pathetic and painful, our response is to circumstances rather than character; it is cerebral rather than visceral. These stories are essentially static and disclose their portraits of entrapment scenically rather than narratively.

In one of Miss Bowen's most masterful performances, "The Little Girl's Room," the situation is established rapidly. Geraldine, twelve, is being reared by her step-grandmother, Mrs. Letherton-Channing, who is "determined to prove [her] a wonder-child." In the elegant Italianate home where Geraldine's mother Vivien refused to bring her and where she "declared that she could never breathe," Geraldine's step-grandmother, "ambushed in gentleness," watches her "for the most tentative ananations of young genius." Initially, then, the story has affinities with Aldous Huxley's famed tale, "Young Archameides." But Miss Bowen's development of Geraldine's situation defies reader anticipation.

The story opens upon a party in progress. Geraldine is having her "moment"; she is passing around the circle with a taper lighting cigarettes, but only later does her association with flame or fire become relevant. In succession, hereafter, Geraldine is seen by herself in the garden; in the study with her Greek tutor, Mr. Scutcheon; and alone in her room with "the Enemies." Any expectation that Geraldine is a cowed child, suppressed and lifeless, is quickly dispatched in the garden scene; for she appears, within the limits of her resources, as a hellion: pulling a rose to pieces "with an obscure sense of triumph," and making up cruel couplets about Mrs. Letherton-Channing's guests ("Old Miss Ellis . . . pink as hell is"). Geraldine is in the garden to keep her tutor waiting. When she is twenty-five minutes late she decides Mr. Scutcheon should be ready, that he "should by now have come to the boil and be cross enough." What follows is what Geraldine considers to be the most interesting hour of her week—creating a calculated but malevolently subtle hell for the Greek tutor. She approaches him "ecstatically, like a martyr approaching a lion." Well aware of his thoughts —"He can't bear me!"—she finds them delicious. Not unsurprisingly, there are also others about who do not care for Geraldine, such as Miss Weekes, the resident lady gardener, and Miss Snipe, the music mistress, beneath whose obsequious manner Geraldine has found, to her satisfaction, enmity.

In a bedroom scene, Geraldine enacts a daily drama, a fantasy of "red passion," in which she alone faces "the Enemy," namely Mr. Scutcheon, Miss Weekes, Miss Snipe, other teachers, and her mother. It is the moment of "revolution," and Vivien tells her "It's all up, Geraldine." As the Enemies confer, "a delicious anticipation" rises in Geraldine; and, as they converge upon her, her excitement, "courted with every sense," becomes orgasmic.

Mrs. Letherton-Channing believes she is providing Geraldine with a glorious opportunity for attaining knowledge and beauty, but these are nothing to the child who possesses a "small intellectual flame. . . ." Not until the end are we fully aware of what else the step-grandmother is providing the child in her "prison": security. The child can torture, both literally and imaginatively, as well as drop off to sleep so readily because "Security, feeling for her in the dark, closed the last of its tentacles on her limbs, her senses." Mrs. Letherton-Channing's dreams for the child are less crushing than corrupting. For example, "Nobody was encouraged to contradict Geraldine: it became penal to hurt her feelings." Geraldine does not possess the hoped-for genius, but the narrative voice suggests that she is a prodigy in another direction, as "a sensationalist." The story leaves an afterglow of anticipation—what deviltry is ahead for the growing Geraldine?

The protagonist of "The Dancing Mistress," Joyce James, twenty-one, mechanically devotes herself six days a week to dance instruction. Constantly tired, she sleeps when she is not teaching. A beautiful girl, she attracts Lulu, a young Swiss who is in England learning the hotel business; but his efforts to stimulate her are ineffective because of her indifference and weariness. Her piano accompanist, Miss Peel, "Peelie," encourages Lulu and tries unsuccessfully to interest Joyce in him. Peelie, who is herself not overly acquainted with life, is rather masculine and aloof; and, constantly cold, she seeks to suck heat from radiators.

The narrator implies that the potential for servitude exists in the respective professions of Joyce and Lulu: "It did not do for Lulu, who shows ladies into their bedrooms, or Joyce who spent hours in clumsy men's arms, to be patently man and woman. . . ." If Lulu will not succumb to this potential, Joyce has. In her background is the shadowy figure of Madame Majowski, her teacher and now employer. Either deliberately, at a younger age, or, more likely, almost unnoticed, Joyce has committed herself to her work until now, "She had eight dancing dresses . . . and besides these and the fur coat to cover them nothing at all but a cloth coat-and-skirt that looked wrong in the country and shabby in town." One of the most telling statements occurs in an exchange between Peelie and Joyce while they are momentarily alone in a dining room where Lulu has brought them:

> "Do wake up," [Peelie] said. "Can't you really love anyone?"
>
> "I didn't want to—you brought me. . . . Well then, give me my powder-puff."
>
> "You've got heaps on—it's colour you want. Haven't you got—"
>
> "No, you know I don't have any; Majowski hates it."

The dialogue is so handled as to shift Joyce's final comment back to Peelie's initial question.

Life will out, however, though surreptitiously if need be. One of Joyce's students is a little girl named Margery Mannering who "never [does] any right." Only Margery has the capacity to evoke feeling in Joyce, and each time Joyce looks at the child she wants to kill her. Her only show of emotion is lashing out at Margery: "The unrealized self in her made itself felt, disturbing her calm with a little shudder of pleasure." The single instance in which Joyce directs any animation toward Lulu occurs when she refers to her encounter: " 'Did you see me killing that child?' she asked Lulu, eagerly turning. 'You were at the door, you must have seen. Wasn't I dreadful—Peelie thinks I was dreadful.' "

Although not as fine a story as those already discussed, "Telling" is worth mentioning because it is perhaps the author's most "absurb" tale. The madness of its humor is correlative to the basic narrative circumstances. In one sense, it is a family story, with the narrator zeroing in on one member, Terry, an inept young man who is out of step with the rest of the family. No allowances are made for him. He is the one whom others ease aside so they can do the job; he is never listened to. Faced with the alternative of defining himself as he is reflected in those about him or breaking through to establish an identity determined by himself and recognized as such, he chooses the latter—and commits murder.

As the story opens, Terry has just killed Josephine in a ruined chapel on the edge of the estate. In the action which follows Miss Bowen shows Terry seeking to communicate his deed to various members of his family and being ignored. At the same time, she cleverly builds up a context which explains why he has been driven to this act. Terry enters his home savoring his knowledge and his new power, but frustration closes in on him quickly enough. He says to a sister,

> "Beatrice, what would you do if I'd killed somebody?"
>
> "Laugh," said she, wearily.

"If I'd killed a woman?"
"Laugh harder. Do you know any women?"

To his brother Charles, Terry says, "You should have seen the blood on my hands just now." His brother replies, "Bad luck!"—and leaves.

In the climatic and concluding scene, Terry seeks out his father in his den. He knows he will convince his father of the deed because he will show him the knife—the murder weapon—which he has in his pocket. But, when the moment arrives to produce the knife, it is not on him. "It *was* here," he cries. He breaks into tears. His father says, "What are you trying to tell me?" Terry replies, "weeping and shaking. 'Nothing, nothing, nothing.'"

A dampish fog-clogged December at a smart but now almost deserted seaside Irish hotel complements the three nonlove stories intertwined in the ironically titled "A Love Story." When one member of a supposed love relationship seeks to fulfill himself or herself, the story suggests the arrangement is bound to be mutually destructive. The marriage of Polly and Clifford Perry-Dunton is the most clear-cut of the three cases. Polly's father has purchased Clifford, who is twenty-four, for his unhappy daughter, thirty-two. Though he comes to the parched nature of Polly like "rain," the marriage is actually the "rape of Clifford." His desire to write and to gain the money and time to find himself as a writer has betrayed him to her wealth. She is a jealous keeper who suffers when he is out of sight; the only thing he really tenders on her investment is obedience. There is a depressing image of him sitting alone in their expensive car, slumped over the wheel, "completely deflated, a dying pig that has died."

The arrival of Mrs. Massey and her daughter Teresa at the hotel from their neighboring home provides the story with its slender line of action. Mrs. Massey found she could not bear to remain in her home after learning of the death of her lover in a World War II battle. Gradually one learns that Teddy, the mother's lover, was really Teresa's contemporary and much more interested in her than in her mother. Mrs. Massey's formidable nature clearly could not countenance this interest when her own heart was set upon Teddy. Teresa later tells another character that her mother would "rather [Teddy] dead than gone from her." His demise seemingly has made public a fact which had previously been true only privately.

Frank Mull, who along with Clifford ends up driving the Masseys back to their home to round off the story, is staying at the hotel with his "cousin" Linda. Frank with "his gusto, his sociability, his human fun, and his conquering bossiness," provides a considerable contrast with the other characters, and he is initially highly decep- tive. But once the nature of his roving eye (he becomes quite taken with Teresa) and his personal views on life—"how foolish it [is], in love, to have to differentiate between women"—are understood, the *ad nauseam* trap he is in becomes apparent. Linda, feeling "quite suspended," patiently endures.

The wife, Janet, in "Foothold" is Miss Bowen's version of a figure treated frequently by D. H. Lawrence—the mind-oriented woman. Janet has a voluptuous body and, it becomes apparent, the sensuous desires it implies, but this part of her being is under "the domination of her clear fastidious aloof mind." It is ironical that, when she seeks a compensatory outlet for her suppressed desires through the creation of a ghost, she projects not a man but a woman, "Clara," with whom to commiserate. The situation sug- gests a Jamesian influence; and, when Janet thinks about another life "waiting the whole time," echoes of a story like "The Jolly Corner" are apparent.

Janet discovers her ghost in the older country home to which she and her husband Gerard have recently moved. Both the husband and wife are preoccupied with Clara when a bachelor friend, Thomas, arrives for a visit and is inevitably drawn into the issue. Gerard, facetious about Clara before Janet, confides his real concern over Janet's state to Thomas: "She's seeing too much of this ghost. . . ." Not unreasonably, Gerard assumes his wife's fantasy relates to their recent move to the country. He tells Thomas, "I didn't reckon on one sort of change, and that seems to have happened. I don't even know if it's something minus or plus."

That the new house has affected Janet is evident enough from her comments to Thomas: "I do feel the house has grown since we've been in it. The rooms seem to take so much longer to get across. I'd no idea we were buying such a large one." This reaction to the house obviously relates to her attempted definition of her new sense of life: "my life—this life—seems to have stretched somehow; there's more room in it." Evidently the larger house and the open surroundings have made Janet conscious at some level of her unfulfilled existence.

Additional comments by Janet establish the static nature of her circumstances. When Thomas asks if her troubles might be due to her not yet having settled in, she replies, "Oh, I've settled down. Settled, I should be surprised to hear, for life." Showing him through the spacious gardens, she adds, "One works here within limitations. There's a character to be kept—you feel that? One would have had greater scope with an older house or a newer house." The story works cleverly with the paradoxical conjunction of roominess and constriction; and their union, as it were, has given birth to Clara.

At the fadeout, Thomas, passing along the hallway outside Janet's bedroom, overhears her saying, "Oh, Clara. . . . How could you bear it? The sickening loneliness. . . ." Thomas's insight into the situation provides a sardonic summation: " 'A peevish dead woman where we've failed . . . it's absurd.' Gerard and he—he thought how much less humiliating for them both it would have been if she'd taken a lover."

"Ivy Gripped the Steps" is a frame story which encompasses a full evocation of a past time. The present Gavin Doddington has been damaged by a past experience which he has never forgotten but which he has never been able to bypass emotionally. In the beginning, he literally returns to the locale which has caused him such pain because it once had brought him such joy. The setting is seaside Southstone in the closing days of World War II. Coastal wartime conditions have hastened the decay which had already come to the street in which the handsome Mrs. Nicholson lived when Gavin came as a delicate boy for two summers. In her day, the street was "one of the best residential avenues" in the city.

In Nathaniel Hawthorne's terms, Gavin has been victimized by the worst of all sins: the manipulation of one human being by another. The sanctity of his heart was invaded by the alluring young widow. His days with Lilian Nicholson were the high point of his young life until the day he overheard a conversation between her and another of her acquaintances and learned he has been "used."

The son of a poor farmer, Gavin is invited to the seaside home for his health because his mother was a girlhood friend of Lilian. Coming from the hard Midland's life, Gavin finds the wealth and style of Lilian's fashionable Southstone exotic. Within the capacities of a young boy, he falls in love with her, and Lilian does nothing to discourage his intense but obviously uncomprehended feelings.

At least in one instance she responds to him as fully as he could wish when she cries, "Why do I stay on and on here; what am I doing? Why don't we go right away somewhere, Gavin; you and I?"

Gavin's traumatic experience occurs when he overhears Admiral Concannon, a married man in whom Lilian has sought to provoke interest in herself, clarifying his position for her:

I see, now, where you are in your element. You know as well as I do what your element is; which is why there's nothing more to be said. Flirtation has always been off my beat—so far off my beat, as a matter of fact, that I didn't know what it was when I first saw it. There, no doubt, I was wrong. If you can't live without it, you cannot, and that is that. If you have to be dangled after, you no doubt will be. But don't, my dear girl, go for that to the wrong shop. It would have been enough, where I am concerned, to watch you making a ninnie of that unfortunate boy."

"Who , poor little funny Gavin?" said Mrs. Nicholson. "Must I have nothing?—I have no little dog."

Gavin, now an aging bachelor, finds Mrs. Nicholson's old home deserted and in the grips of ivy: "The process of strangulation could be felt . . ."; and, "one could have convinced oneself that the ivy must be feeding on something inside the house." Appropriately, the word "gripped" is also linked with Gavin to describe the nature of his living: "Despair, the idea that his doom must be never, never to reach her, not only now but ever, gripped him and gripped his limbs. . . ." Gavin's experience links him, of course, with the young heroines of the novels whose romantic dreams are shattered and betrayed by the adult world. But Gavin's betrayal is carried to its uttermost conclusion; the death that Emmeline suffers in *To the North* is to be preferred to the lifetime of hell endured by Gavin who has "the face of somebody dead who [is] still there . . . under an icy screen, of a whole stopped mechanism for feeling."

"The Disinherited" is both one of Miss Bowen's longest stories and one of her most detailed depictions of corruption. At the center of the narrative is Davina Archworth, twenty-nine, who is "idle with a melancholy and hollow idleness. . . ." Without money or life of her own, she has come to live off an elderly aunt whose house sits on a rise overlooking a university town. This situation brings Davina into contact with two others, Prothero, Mrs. Archworth's chauffeur, and Marianne Harvey, a quiet "modern" wife who lives in one of many new homes being built on an estate above the town.

Underlying the story is the theme of mutability. The season is autumn, appropriate to the images of decay which abound; the atmosphere is decadent. Davina takes takes Marianne to a surreptitious party at a big house where the owner is absent, where mustiness abounds, and where there are no bulbs in the grand saloon because the owner is "as poor as a rat." Much is also made of the rawness of the new housing development; it is without lawns, but with "half made roads, like the first knowing cuts of a scalpel. . . ." At the very close of the story, when Davina has been walking by herself and has decided to leave her aunt's and move on, though she has no place to go, she watches as "two men came uphill her way, stopped and debated: they were surveyors coming to peg out a new road." Times are changing, and Davina finds herself neither a member in good standing of the old order nor a candidate for the new. One of the disinherited, she is like the grass on the new homes estate: "wiry grass that had lost its nature, being no longer meadow and not yet lawn."

Davina sees herself as an aristocrat without the means. She believes it is money she wants, though it is more likely power. She began with money, but "love affairs and her other expensive habits had ruined her." The thought of money pulses through her mind like the undercurrent chanting of "There must be more money" which recurs in D. H. Lawrence's most telling tale of money madness, "The Rocking-Horse Winner." The narrator says of Davina: "Her thoughts were almost all angry. 'If I had money—' she said again and again."

It is money which brings her into close contact with Prothero. Offering kisses in return, she borrows from him. He too is corrupt, and almost instinctively she recognizes him as a criminal. Like her, Prothero can not have what he wants; and his story comments upon hers and suggests that her disinheritance is not simply material or sociological but is also psychological. Prothero once had an affair with a married woman whom he loved to distraction; but she came to spurn him and, in his agony and frustration, he smothered her. Now he spends his evenings writing letters to her of purported disdain, which are betrayed by anguished postscripts, "Anita I love you Anita, Anita where are you?. . . come back, where are you, I won't hurt you, come back, come back, come back—"

The borrowing of money from Prothero and the kisses are simply a measure of Davina's decay. At one point in the story she says, "I hate having no power." Near the close, she threatens

Prothero with dismissal; but he already has "too much on her."
She has no power over even the likes of him. Hers is, and will
continue to be, a study in self-betrayal.

The only person Davina can manipulate is Marianne, who is,
initially at least, flattered by Davina's attention. To Davina,
Marianne's life and new home are "mullish," and the whole housing
development is "hygienic and intellectual." For her part,
Marianne loves her home, is proud of it, and is a serene wife of
"mild good spirits." Her husband, Matthew, fifteen years her
senior, is another who is conscious of change: " . . . he saw how his
friends grew grayer, how their sentiments creaked, and, with dismay
for himself, dreaded to desiccate. He clung to his wife's ever-
freshness, her touch of the vine leaf." The Harveys have two sons
away at school.

The story's major dramatic scene is the party to which Davina
takes Marianne while her husband is in London. Her limited
contact with Davina has already infected her: "Marianne's heart
was set on this evening's pleasure, this fantastic setting-out. In
these weeks of knowing Davina her faculty for disapproval seemed
to be all used up. She was under a spell." Yet it is clear she is not
completely benumbed, for at the start and recurringly throughout
the subsequent adventures of the evening, she "wished herself
safe at home." The party is composed of a motley crew, Davina's
crowd, of men and women who are also caught between desire and
impossibility of fulfillment. Principal among them is Oliver, the
man with whom Davina was once in love and who is to seduce
Marianne before the party's end. He exists by cataloguing the li-
braries of big homes and hence his presence at "Lord
Thingummy's" and the possibility for the party in the Lord's
absence. As with Davina, "the old order left him stranded, the new
offered him no place." For Oliver, the stout Purdon, the oldish
platinum blonde Miriam, and the others, the party is little more
than an occasion for the sharing of mutual pain. The images imply
they are in hell: "Now, each immobile from poverty, each frozen
into their settings like leaves in the dull ice of different puddles,
they seldom met." Such descriptives as "horrid," "empty,"
"askew," "bald," "vacuity," "yawning," "chill," "peevish,"
"muffled," "tarnished," and "congested" pile up.

Oliver, "a broken-spirited Viking," wanders off through the house
with an uncertain Marianne. Eventually, he cries for her, and he

seemingly seduces her. As he recollects the next morning, "he had unwillingly, deluded her with tears. . . ." In a nice touch, the story gives the scene the following day in which Marianne meets her husband at the station and returns home with him. The occasion is typical of Miss Bowen in its elliptical, tense, and deliciously suggestive nature. Having settled into the living room, Matthew says, "I think . . . I must get my glasses changed! 'Changed?' said Marianne, starting." What we are left speculating about is the impact of the previous night upon Marianne's future. She is conscious of change, and Matthew detects something: " 'What's the matter?' he said. 'You're not quite yourself.' 'Perhaps I have got a slight chill.' " Mutability, then, both physical and metaphysical, is the way of life. Among Miss Bowen's shorter fiction, "The Disinherited" is one of her most telling portrayals of the pain change can inflict—and of the human incapacity for adapting to it.

II *Purgatorial Possibilities*

Everyone has met people whom he would love to shake or shock in some manner—people who are complacent, self-righteous, self-satisfied, or self-important. Miss Bowen shares these impulses, and a group of her stories shows her administering some artistic shaking up. At the center of each of these tales is an individual whose attitudes to or whose views about life are called into question. The action revolves around an "opportunity" presented to him for self-discovery or self-judgment. Generally, the opportunity comes suddenly in the form of a shock—a mental or emotional jolt designed to be salutary. As with each grouping, stories typical of my generalizations (such as "The Working Party") give way to skillful variations. In "The Jungle," for example, the challenge to a particular outlook is cumulative rather than sudden. "Shoes: An International Episode" enjoys a particularly sardonic ending for the very reason that the administered attack proves insufficient to unseat the resident smugness. One of Miss Bowen's best stories, the frequently anthologized "The Queen Heart," displays a most astute switch and gains force by confronting the reader with a complex problem of judgment; the character under attack is wonderfully appealing, and the individuals surrounding her are otherwise.

"The Working Party" is the intersection of two events. The first is Mrs. Fisk's entertaining of the local sewing circle in her large farm home. She is twenty-one, a recent bride, and unknowing about life. Wrapped up in herself, she is complacent, egotistical, and willful. This occasion is the first time she entertains the ladies, and she is determined to outdo all of their afternoons which she has attended. Her preparations are elaborate. Since her husband and his men are to be working in a distant field, "she and the Working Party are to be absolutely alone." By the time the ladies arrive, of course, Mrs. Fisk is tense, pulled between "apprehension and pleasure." When some of the ladies begin talking about Mrs. Fisk's deceased mother-in-law, recalling her difficulties, Mrs. Fisk tosses her chin and adds, "*I've* had no difficulties." The vicar's wife assures her she is most fortunate, "and her tone [says]: 'That is not the lot of the human soul . . . that is not the lot of woman.' " The buildup leaves us anticipating trouble; there can be no doubt that, as Mrs. Fisk patronizes the ladies, her moment for "attack" is propitious.

This shock arrives on schedule to challenge Mrs. Fisk's egotistical lack of awareness and to expose her essential inhumanity. The unforeseen event is the death of the Fisk's cowherd Cottesby, whose body she finds slumped against the wall at the bottom of the short flight of stairs leading to the kitchen. Since his death is not really unexpected, it lacks the force of sudden surprise; Cottesby has had "a heart" for years and was threatened with death intermittently. Even so, we are not prepared for her defiant reaction of "What of it?" Though certainly unsettled, her determination to make the tea party a success stiffens her. And, finding her cook Phyllis crying in the kitchen and neglecting her duties gives her further bolstering reason to think, "nothing should wreck her."

The party proper progresses smoothly, but Mrs. Fisk's subconscious begins to churn away. When the Vicar's wife wonders if she still has the former Mrs. Fisk's beautiful copper preserving pans, Mrs. Fisk begins to imagine the Vicar's wife "walking about the house . . . opening and shutting doors." Then she has an image of ladies laying out Cottesby on her kitchen table. She is resoundingly recalled to reality by several cups proferred for more tea— only to discover her urn empty. The plans for Phyllis to appear with more hot water at the midpoint in the party have gone awry. Rising to fetch more water, Mrs. Fisk, shaken, maintains an appearance of composure until she quits her parlor. Suddenly she finds she cannot go down the stairs past the dead man. Quitting the house, she flees across the fields in search of her husband. When she sees him, she cries out her anguish. The closing sentence is: "She had forgotten the Working Party."

Alban, of "Her Table Spread," is a peculiarly modern young man. He is aware that "some spring had dried up at the root of the world." Consequently, he has little feeling for love: "his attitude to women was negative." He feels no attraction at all for Valeria Cuffe, the wealthy young woman who has invited him to her castle on the coast of Ireland. She has had thoughts of marrying him, though he is not handsome. In fairness to Alban, Valeria's mannerisms are disconcerting. She is wealthy, she is handsome—"of statuesque development"—but she is "still detained in childhood."

On the evening of Alban's arrival at the castle, he is attracted both by the elegance of Valeria's gown and those of two older ladies who are present and by the impressive table which has been laid. He links the display with himself and concludes that a young man from London is an occasion for them; but he soon learns that in the estuary below a destroyer is anchored. Some months previously, at a time when Valeria was absent, another destroyer had paused in the estuary, and the officers (including one named Garrett) had come ashore to be entertained at supper in the neighborhood. Valeria has convinced herself that officers will climb the hill this night to her castle—all is in readiness for them.

The evening is wet, and no one appears. Valeria excuses herself, and the next thing Alban and the other guests know, she is standing on the brow of the hill in the rain waving a great lantern up and down. Old Mr. Rossiter, with Alban following, heads for the boat-house to stand guard. As he observes, "She might come for the boat; she's a fine oar. . . ." During their chat in the boathouse, Rossiter drops a key observation about Valeria which may well register with Alban: "She's a girl you could shape." Meanwhile, Valeria's imagination is working overtime. The wit of the story is adroit and culminative and hence difficult to illustrate briefly; but the following passage, embracing Valeria's viewpoint, gives a sense of it:

When he and she were married (she inclined a little to Mr. Garrett) they would invite all the Navy up the estuary and give them tea. Her estuary would be filled up, like a regatta, with loud excited battleships tooting to one another and flags flying. The terrace would be covered with grateful sailors, leaving room for the band. She would keep the peacocks her aunt did not allow. His friends would be surprised to notice that Mr. Garrett

had meanwhile become an admiral, all gold. He would lead the other
admirals into the castle and say, while they wiped their feet respectfully:
"These are my wife's statues; she has given them to me. One is Mars, one is
Mercury. We have a Venus, but she is not dressed. And wait till I show you
our silver and gold plates. . . ." The Navy would be unable to tear itself
away.

As Alban leaves Rossiter to climb the hill and return to the castle,
he is mistaken in the dark for an officer. Valeria cries out to the
other ladies, "Mr. Garrett has landed." Alban looks up through the
rain: "[Valeria] laughed like a princess, magnificently justified.
Their unseen faces were all three lovely, and, in the silence after the
laughter, such a strong tenderness reached him that, standing there
in full manhood, he was for a moment not exiled. For the moment,
without moving or speaking, he stood, in the dark, in a flame, as
though all three said: 'My darling. . . .' "
The unspoken thought is typical of many Bowen endings; a direction is indicated but not forced. The author is too scrupulous to
insist upon firm resolutions. Here, Alban has been touched at a new
depth for him. We cannot say if his future holds Valeria; but he
can never be quite the same again. And that is good.
In "Shoes: An International Episode," Dillie and Edward Aherne,
wed two years, are vacationing at a small hotel in France. The story
is largely a good-natured and detailed portrait of them as a couple.
They are likable in many ways, but they are of a limited and complacent outlook: they are trapped, really, by the belief that their
frankness and openness make them knowing and wise. They think
themselves modern, and this satisfies them.
The narrative element is their "challenge," but the point of the
story is that, while this assault provides an emotional crisis of sorts,
it is absorbed. This tale is of opportunity missed. On the morning
in question, Edward retrieves their shoes from the hallway; but the
lady's shoes are not Dillie's. Her proper brogues (size six and a half,
though she likes size seven for real comfort) have been replaced by
what she calls "the Horrors," very high heels, fawn kid with red
trim, size three. The day's conversation weaves in and around the
topic of the brogues versus "the Horrors," the attempts to retrieve
Dillie's shoes, her tossing of "the Horrors" out her bedroom
window, and so forth. Edward's obvious admiration for the "sexy"
shoes unsettles Dillie. She cries, "Oh, Edward, what a conception of

women!" She is distressed by the thought that "no men really want to respect women."

There are moments when it appears Dillie will reassess herself. When she and Edward are inspecting a cathedral, she comments: "Has one got a terribly little soul? How could one have felt shoes mattered?" But she reverts quickly enough to the defensive and to slighting accusations of the French about her. She operates by clearly defined conceptions of herself and clichés. She treats Edward, for example, with "calculated amiability" and retains a horror of being a "wee wifey." The moment of shock should register when the hotel boy Anatole arrives at the door with her brogues and proffers them, saying, "*V'la des chaussures de Monsieur.*" The narrator observes that "It was the moment, certainly, for Dillie to make a demonstration." Neither demonstration nor any self-illumination is forthcoming: "*was* Anatole worth it—so small, so sleek. . .?"; and the brogues, after all, have "no nonsense about them." Dillie is safe and so too is amiable, dense Edward. Equipped with her brogues and ready to collect more cathedrals, Dillie is off again with husband in tow. Leaving their room, they "clattered down the corridor, disturbing some dozen siestas. Talking loudly together about the Latin mentality, they passed with a blink and a gasp. . . ."

Even if a fifteen-year-old schoolgirl appears as an unlikely inhabitant of Purgatory, "The Jungle" fits the general configuration of this grouping. It might more properly be termed a "growing-up" story, for Rachel Ritchie's unformed personality and limited concepts are shaken and stretched through contact with athletic, self-possessed Elise Lamartine. Rachel, an imaginative girl, is delighted when she discovers through some hedgerows and over a fence near her school a wild area which she christens "the Jungle." "An absolutely neglected and wild place," it functions in part as a correlative for Elise. Rachel's "Jungle" brings "a funny lurch" to her imagination just as Elise does to her life.

From a very proper family, Rachel is a sensitive, quiet, nonassertive girl. She is liked well enough by other girls who nevertheless find her easy to forget "unintentionally." Thus, to acquire a friend who says "damn" and whose family never eats late dinner but supper, opens up a new range of possibilities for Rachel. After the pair, for example, is punished for arriving late at chapel, Rachel, "usually humiliated by punishment, went about feeling clever and daring."

It is incorrect, however, to suggest, as the above summation may, that this is a story of friendship per se. This adroitly amusing work is largely concerned with Rachel's struggle to accept friendship on what are largely Elise's terms. In conflict, so far as it affects Rachel, are her pride and concepts of what should be, and Elise's trying and seemingly indifferent "independence." At one point, after Rachel has accused her of being bossy, Elise retorts, "I never take any notice of anybody unless I happen to like them, and if they think I'm bossy I can't help it." Rachel's problems with Elise, given the school context, are delightfully compounded by the fact that Elise is a year behind Rachel. Not only must Rachel endure remarks from classmates but also from mistresses who refer to "going about with the younger ones." Elise helps not at all by always swaggering ahead of Rachel and by throwing back over her shoulder "without even looking: 'Buck up: do come on!' "

The strain is too great, and Rachel draws back. Elise displays no apparent concern; she has her own friend, and is on the school eleven ("no one under fifteen had ever got their colours before"). For Rachel it is otherwise. The term has progressed to the point where the rest of the girls have established their twosomes and threesomes. Rachel, left on her own, decides "It really hadn't been much of a term." But, near the end of the school year, she slips off alone to the Jungle, not having been there since the one time she took Elise and, with an especially proprietary attitude, introduced her to it. There she finds Elise fast asleep.

Only gradually in "The Inherited Clock" does one become aware of the poor relationship that Clara Detter has with her own past. She has, unconsciously rather than deliberately, obliterated painful experiences from her memory—an act which leaves her psyche inchoate. Her inheritance of a skeleton clock (a clock without a face and with all of the works showing under a removable glass dome) brings about a mental crisis which she does not comprehend but which must be resolved if her sanity is to survive. Necessarily, much of the story is expository in nature and is skillfully revealed more or less simultaneously to Clara and the reader. The chronology of the narrative is highly fragmented, and the resulting kaleidoscopic effect dramatically conveys the mental confusion and stress gripping Clara.

Clara and her second cousin, Paul Ardeen, have been exploited by their maiden aunt, Rosanna Detter. When they were infants,

Rosanna declared them her heirs. They accordingly grew up with great expectations, but, with "no allowances and few presents," they lived in cramped financial circumstances. From childhood onward, enmity between Clara and Paul increased, fostered if anything by the highly amused Rosanna who played one against the other. When the aunt died, Clara was thirty; Paul, two or three years older. By this time, Paul has gained full insight into the whole sorry situation, and he gives Clara the benefit of his perception in the closing scene. Rosanna, like them, was left anticipating wealth for years. Among other things, her wait cost her the one possible love of her life. Paul tells Clara, "You and I were her fun. Can't you see how things worked out? The younger the heirs you name, the longer they have to wait, and the more the waiting can do to them."

The traumatic day of Clara's life occurred when she was six and was with Paul visiting Rosanna at her estate home, Sandyhill. Symbolically and perversley, Rosanna's prize possession is the skeleton clock; and on this day, after Paul tells her how much he would like to have it, she says "Yes, I dare say you would" and then informs Clara it is to be hers. Paul in his recapitulation has an answer for this decision as well: "I was a man, so she liked my going without." At any rate, Clara does indeed inherit the clock which is supposed to have run continuously for over a hundred years. But for some reason Clara finds the clock truly unsettling, though she cannot grasp why this should be so. As she tells Paul, "This seems to be like a whole continent that's submerged, you know."

After Rosanna told the child Clara that the clock was to be hers, the angered Paul had removed the glass bell from it and had tricked Clara into sticking her fingers into the workings by asking her, "Have you ever SEEN a minute: Have you actually had one wriggling inside your hand?" In the afterminutes, Clara was not troubled by her bruised and bleeding finger; but she was terrified by the stoppage of the clock. Paul sent her out into the garden to detain Rosanna and her other visitors while he sought to restart the clock. The story opens with the suggestive garden scene, the import of which is only subsequently disclosed.

At the climax, Paul acts to save Clara and to gain the clock he has long coveted. He restages the earlier scene of removing the bell and sticking Clara's finger into the workings saying, "Either this works . . . or I take you by hand tomorrow to a psychiatrist." The experiment does work, and Clara is released into an integrated being by acquiring her true inheritance of a hitherto suspended past. She tells Paul, "I shall sit with my memories. I expect to spend some time getting to know them." And then she offers the clock to him. He accepts, but he asks if he may leave it with her for the present since he has no place for it.

Mrs. Cadman of "The Queer Heart" is the most fully evoked character in Miss Bowen's short fiction—and also one of the most trying to judge. Stout, good-natured, not inclined to worry, she has lived a happy life, enjoyed herself, found happiness with her equally easygoing husband, who is now deceased. As first introduced to us, she seems perfectly harmless: we smile at her as do several fellow passengers on her bus, and we understand why she is considered something of a character. Gradually, the story uncovers the wider implications of her life and nature.

The occasion of the story is her sister Rosa's visit to Mrs. Cadman and her grown daughter Lucille. This older sister, who is in her stringent manner, antithetical to Mrs. Cadman has taken to such semiannual trips only since the death of Mr. Cadman, who did not care for her dour outlook. Mrs. Cadman does not enjoy these visits since her severe daughter, normally tolerable to live with, and Rosa join forces to criticize her. This time not only has Rosa come, but she has taken seriously ill; and, if Lucille is correct, she is on the verge of death.

When Mrs. Cadman is seen in her house, it becomes necessary to revise the initial assessment of her. It is evident, finally, that both Rosa and Lucille are a consequence of Mrs. Cadman's life. Lucille suffers in her sensitivity because her mother's public appearance and conduct are a constant source of embarrassment, while her self-indulgent ways absorb her capacity for love. The mother-daughter relationship exists in reverse. Mrs. Cadman's sheepishness, her piggishness with candy, and her banging of doors are all reminiscent of a child rather than of an aging woman. Her face, in fact, is "as ingenuous as a little girl's," while her vanity over tight pumps is girlish.

The key scene is a confrontation between the sisters. Mrs. Cadman seeks to avoid a bedside visit as she has most likely sidestepped anything unpleasant all her life. In a way, we can empathize with Mrs. Cadman since Rosa proves a bitter individual whose lifelong jealousy and self-righteous attitude to her sister have corroded her. In this interview, Rosa reveals when and why she first consciously assumed her rigid stance. When both were little children one Christmastime, Mrs. Cadman had asked for and received a doll Rosa had longed to have. Recounting the scene of which Mrs. Cadman has no recollection, Rosa, quite unappealingly says, "I could have fretted, seeing you take everything. One thing, then another. But I was shown. God taught me to pity you." The scene brings some measure of insight to Mrs. Cadman; for she thinks, "I did that to her; then what have I done to Lucille?"

Mrs. Cadman has lived the unexamined life, symbolized perhaps by her act of backing off the bus; but there is uncertainty as to the extent she may be blamed. She has been akin to the blue-eyed, golden-haired people Thomas Mann's protagonists admire and long to be. Rosa recalls her younger sister's great beauty and popularity: "They were taken with you." Mrs. Cadman also has affinities with Dinah Delecroix of *The Little Girls* who, by virtue of her attractiveness, has been well looked after and allowed to bypass the humanizing shocks of life.

Different as it is in subject matter, D. H. Lawrence's fine story, "Odour of Chrysanthemums," is very close to the final configuration of "The Queer Heart." Mrs. Cadman's illumination before Rosa parallels that of Elizabeth Bates before her dead husband's body.

III *Divine Madness*

Few short-story themes have proven more fruitful for Miss Bowen than that of dislocation. Sensitive people, she observes, do not suffer the disintegration of their world lightly; they frequently react, seemingly involuntarily, in strange and unexpected ways when it is threatened. The irrational within appears to answer the call of chaos and of the irrational without; or, as Miss Bowen has said, "one counteracts fear with fear, stress with stress." Miss Bowen had employed the theme of dislocation earlier; but, with the coming of World War II, it fully engaged her imagination. The stories written in wartime London and published as *The Demon Lover* have dislocation as their major concern. In the Preface to the American edition of the collection, Miss Bowen characterizes the climate of bomb-wracked London and the psychological problems of its residents: " . . . I do not think that the desiccation, by war, of our day-to-day lives can be enough stressed. The outside world war news was stupefying: headlines and broadcasts came down and down on

us in hammer-like chops, with great impact but oddly little rever-
beration. The simple way to put it was: 'One cannot take things in.'
What was happening was out of all proportion to our faculties for
knowing, thinking and checking up" (*Afterthought*, 49).

At issue for the individual was the preservation of a sense of self:
"You used to know what you were from the things you liked, and
chose. Now there was not what you liked, and you did not choose"
(49). This effort to survive sometimes resulted in hallucinatory
experiences—"strange growths"—emanating from the oddest cor-
ners of the psyche; for, as Miss Bowen adds, "Every writer during
this time was aware of the passionate attachment of men and women
to every object or image or place or love of fragment of memory
with which his or her destiny seemed to be assured" (50). Peculiar
behavior or psychological aberrations on the part of individuals
"mechanized by the controls of wartime, and emotionally torn and
impoverished by change," are not to be viewed as self-destructive;
instead, they "are an unconscious, instinctive, saving resort. . ."
(49). Thus we may speak of these responses to overwhelming pressure as divine madness.

"Summer Night," which appeared as the last story in Miss Bowen's
predecessor to *The Demon Lover*, *Look at All Those Roses*(1941),
is especially interesting because it so evidently foreshadows her
wartime stories. In *The Heat of the Day*, a character remarks, "War,
if you come to think of it, hasn't started anything that wasn't there
already . . . ," a statement anticipated by and substantiated in
"Summer Night" (31). Although set in rural Ireland, the story's
characters are very conscious of the war. On the evening of the
story, several of them act in ways that are unique for them, so that
their immoral or irrational responses appear as a counterpart to the
murderous air battles not far distant.

Emma, mother of two, leaves her country home in the family car,
ostensibly to visit relatives but really for an assignation with a man
named Robinson. The story includes scenes of the home she has
left behind; scenes at Robinson's house, where he is entertaining
unexpected visitors; and others showing Emma and Robinson together. It is evident Emma is confronting adultery for the first time,
and it is also clear she has undergone considerable debate as to
whether or not she will visit Robinson in his "china house." She
comes to Robinson in a romantic frame of mind, but his evident
experience and businesslike attitude quickly enough dissipate this

attitude. What began as a "pilgrimage" became an "adventure," and it is simply to end as an affair in a sterile setting: "There was no moon, but dry, tense, translucent darkness: no dew fell."

Robinson's visitors before Emma's arrival have been Justin Cavey, an intellectual, fortyish city bachelor, who is holidaying with his deaf older sister Queenie, and the latter. A perhaps oversensitive person, Justin normally spends his vacations traveling on the Continent. Now, thinking of "the war broken towers of Europe," he suffers: "In the heart of the neutral Irishman indirect suffering pulled like a crooked knife." The ravages of war and the makeshift vacation have disclosed propensities within him hitherto dormant.

Having met Robinson casually to begin with, Justin feels a strong attraction to him: Robinson, he decides, has "on him the touch of some foreign sun." Robinson, a factory manager who drives a high-powered car, is separated from his wife and is regarded as a Blue-beard by the local women; and he is the very antithesis of Justin. Nevertheless, Justin is impelled by Robinson's presence "into all sorts of aberrations of talk and mind . . . as though this type of creature had been a woman. . . ." Justin is drawn "like a perverse person in love, to expose all his own piques, crotchets and weaknesses."

While conversing at Robinson's home, Justin seeks to share with the other man his belief in the need for new modes of thinking and feeling. He sounds very much like Rupert Birkin addressing Gerald Critch in Lawrence's *Women in Love*. Revealingly, Justin tells Robinson that "this war's an awful illumination; it's destroyed our dark; we have to see where we are." Like Critch, Robinson is largely impenetrable; and Justin's comments hardly register with him. When he later sees Robinson and Queenie side by side, he sees they are both against him: "She does not hear with her ears, he does not hear with his mind. No wonder they can communicate." Appropriately, Robinson, the mechanical and abstract man, and Queenie, living in her own world of romantic dreams, are the only contented characters in the story. They are impervious to the climate of the war, just as they are impervious to all pressures. They are, in effect, the natural, thoughtless betrayers of the civilized world.

After Justin and Queenie leave Robinson, Justin, who is aware of a woman sitting in the car in his driveway and awaiting their departure, returns to his room and writes Robinson an angry letter. Though he knows Robinson will be "indifferent" to it, he feels the act of expression is necessary for his own self-preservation. Justin is aware of the relationship between his feelings and the *Zeitgeist*: "You cannot fail to misunderstand what I mean when I say that a year ago this might not have happened to me. But—the assumptions on which I acted, Robinson, are becoming more general in a driven world than you yet (or may ever) know. The extremity to which we are each driven must be the warrant for what we do and say."

Meanwhile at Emma's home, her young daughter Vivie has risen from her bed, removed her nightgown, and raced about naked, her senses feeling the anarchy in the house and "wanting to run the night." She takes colored chalk and tattoos "her chest, belly and thighs with stars and snakes, red, yellow and blue." The child's appearance and conduct send her father's aged Aunt Fran to bed believing "The blood of the world is poisoned. . . ." Troubled as well by Emma's departure, her own outburst against Emma's husband, the Major, the old woman asks herself: "What is the matter tonight—is there a battle?" And she also thinks that "Each moment is everywhere, it holds the war in its crystal; there is no elsewhere, no other place. Not a benediction falls on this apart house of the Major; the enemy is within it, creeping about. Each heart here falls to the enemy." The Major, whose slight physical being belies his appelation, provides a final irony. Preoccupied and worried about the war almost to the point of trance, he has yet to see any connection between the public and private worlds. While he is being cuckolded, he locks up the house, thinking, "it's all right. . . ."

The opening story in *The Demon Lover* is "In the Square," which is a modest yet apt introduction to the material to follow. It establishes in a more normative manner than the remaining stories the radical difference to London that the war has made when the era is compared with the preceding years. Such is conveyed by a quartet of characters in a fashionable London square home during the lapse of a few minutes. If the story had a motto, it would be, "If you can't beat them, join them." Rupert, an old friend, has called to see Magdela at her home after learning that she has returned to London in the wake of reduced bombing. Through them is evoked a sense of the square's earlier years and of the gay, mannered parties of the 1920's and 1930's. Rupert quite clearly remembers with fondness, these splendid social occasions and wishes them back. Contrastingly, Magdela has put the past, if somewhat uneasily, behind her. She implies what other Bowen characters in the novels are fond of saying, "One must live as one can." She sees that now the only possibilities for life reside in adapting to present conditions. A telephone call from a man other than her husband gives a sense of how her life now reflects the immoral conditions of the war.

The other two characters extend the nature of the new era. Magdela is tolerating under her roof a younger woman, Gina, who occupied the house in the earlier years of the war while Magdela was living in the North, and who is, as Madgela knows, her husband's mistress. A social upstart, brittle and capable, Gina represents a new experience for this home. She is an early fictional harbinger of actual social changes realized in England following the war. The fourth character is Bennet, seventeen and Magdela's nephew, who is stopping over en route to his school. He is a cocky, confident young man complete with cigarettes, which Magdela does not approve of but accepts. Having no past at all, he is the least inhibited member of the group. That he should take a bath at six in the evening puzzles even Gina. The flip, sparring remarks exchanged by Bennet and Gina before he leaves the house contrast markedly with the cultivated conversation of the older pair.

As the brief story ends, Rupert and Magdela are standing on the balcony casting nostalgic glances across the square. Magdela says, "Now the place seems to belong to everyone. One has nothing but one's feelings. Sometimes I think I hardly know myself." Magdela foreshadows the protagonists of succeeding stories, except that they, finding themselves threatened more severely, react more radically.

The title story of *The Demon Lover* is typical of several other items in the collection because the protagonist is a woman whose mind reverts to a highly localized past. "The Demon Lover" is a ghost story which builds up and then culminates like an Alfred Hitchcock movie. A woman, in London for the day, stops briefly at her closed London home. The woman is Mrs. Kathleen Drover, who "went round to her shut-up house for several things she wanted to take away." Surprisingly, a letter addressed to her awaits her on the hall table. This is strange on two counts: her mail is now directed by the post office to her country address; no one knew she would be calling at the house this day. The enclosed message staggers Mrs. Drover.

In an inset scene from the past, Kathleen is with her soldier fiancée in August, 1914; it is evening, and they are saying goodbye in a garden. In the context of the story, some of the soldier's comments carry an ominous ring: " 'I shall be with you,' he said, 'sooner or later. You won't forget that. You need do nothing but wait.' " Several years pass before Kathleen marries William Drover. This past provides a context for the letter which Mrs. Drover finds awaiting her with the date of the current day, though in the story the letter dramatically precedes the flashback: "Dear Kathleen: You will not have forgotten that today is our anniversary, and the day we said. The years have gone by at once slowly and fast. In view of the fact that nothing has changed, I shall rely upon you to keep your promise. I was sorry to see you leave London, but was satisfied that you would be back in time. You may expect me, therefore, at the hour arranged. Until then. . . ."

Stunned by this letter signed "K," and caught up in "rapidly heightening apprehension," she cries: "The hour arranged. . . . My God . . . *what* hour? How should I . . . ? After twenty-five years. . . ." The narrator observes: "The desuetude of her former bedroom, her married London home's whole air of being a cracked cup from which memory, with its reassuring power had either evaporated or leaked away, made a crisis—and at just this crisis the letter-writer had, knowledgeably, struck." That she may not be alone occurs to Mrs. Drover; but, as a dependable mother and wife, she determines not to return to her family without the items she has come to fetch. She decides to slip out, get a cab, and bring the driver back to the house with her while she collects what is wanted.

Cautiously, she leaves the house and finds a single taxi waiting in the taxi rank at the corner. She climbs in, and the taxi begins to move off. Mrs. Drover taps on the glass—the driver turns around: "Through the aperture driver and passenger, not six inches between them, remained for an eternity eye to eye. Mrs. Drover's mouth hung open for some seconds before she could issue her first scream. After that she continued to scream and to beat with her gloved hands on the glass all around as the taxi accelerating without mercy, made off with her into the hinterland of deserted streets."

London is not under bombardment by the Germans in "Mysterious Kôr," but by an intense moon which represents an "unreal" threat and, as such, is "perhaps more than senses and nerves could bear." The youthful soldier Arthur (incidentally, the only uniformed

character in *The Demon Lover*) is starting a leave and is wandering
the streets with his girl Pepita. They have no place to spend their
evening, or they at least do not choose to spend it in the tiny flat
Pepita shares with Callie. Pepita, torn between gratefulness to
Callie for her willingness to take in Arthur as an overnight guest
and anger that she has not made arrangements to vacate the flat
for them, knows her girlfriend will await them with cocoa and
"three-sided chat," to be followed by "turning in: that would be
that, and that would be all." Pepita characterizes Callie as "more
slow-witted than narrow-minded. . . ."

The story, which turns upon the contrasting young women,
compares their two forms of unreality. Callie's response to life,
love, and the moonlight is romantic, and links her with the innocent
heroines which appear in Miss Bowen's novels. Pepita's response
to the limitations of existing life might also be construed as highly
romantic, but Miss Bowen's intent is to distinguish her imaginative
adjustment, her superreality, from Callie's unreality.

From a remembered fragment of poetry, Pepita has seized upon
the image of the mysterious, abiding city of Kôr. As she and Arthur
stand looking at ghostly, moon-drenched London, she informs him
of her saving concept. Arthur tells her that he assumed "girls
thought about people." " 'What, these days?' she said. 'Think about
people? How can anyone think about people if they've any heart?' "
Kôr for Pepita is not an ideal which provides an escape from reality;
it is a reality which opposes the unreal chaos of her world. She
quotes from the poem, "The world is disenchanted," to explain why
the poet conceived of it. At a time when "they thought they had
got everything taped, because the whole world had been explored
. . . . Everything and place had been found and marked on some
map," the poet had craved a place created by men but preserved
from man. To the person who hates present civilization, as Pepita
does, Kôr has the added attraction of having no history.

Callie, oblivious of Pepita's actual anguish at being unable to
sleep with Arthur, thinks the moonlight must be wonderful for the
lovers. She fails, after the couple arrives at the flat, to understand
Pepita's angry reaction to her question, "Do you think Arthur's got
all he wants?" Callie's exposure to the lovers and her later chat
with Arthur, when Pepita is asleep, brings about "the loss of her
own mysterious expectations. . . ." As she opens a window, Arthur
asks, "And how's your moon?" It has already faded, and "To Callie

it seemed likely that there would never be such a moon again; and
on the whole she thought this was for the best." We are left to
ponder where she will discover reality, and if she too will take up
citizenship in Kôr with its Byzantium-like sanity and permanency.

The central intelligence of "The Happy Autumn Fields" is a
young woman, Mary. She is another of *The Demon Lover* protagonists who seek salvation from the pressures of wartime London by
almost involuntary theatrics of the mind. Mary has returned to the
bomb-weakened residence that was home before the blitz, despite
the protestations of her fiancée, Travis. She has returned to seek—
what? Travis half understands and half does not, but he is correct
when he tells her, "You don't like it here. Your self doesn't like
it." But it is evident he lacks full insight into her action when he
adds, "Your will keeps driving your self, but it can't be driven the
whole way—it makes its own get out: sleep." Mary is one of Miss
Bowen's chief illustrations of "fighting fear with fear." Evidently
her personally recognizable inner being has been dissipated in her
own eyes through the depersonalization resulting from sharing in
community tension. The return "home" signifies her deep-felt
need to possess and experience a private emotional life. This she
acquires vicariously and, in so doing, gains not the "sleep" anticipated by Travis but the awakeness resulting from a fresh sense of
self.

Home, with its own private store of history and drama, aids Mary
by casting before her an old box of letters dating from mid-Victorian
times. Mary's mind seizes upon this correspondence as a script for
the drama she creates in her mind. We are well into the story of a
memorable day in the life of a well-to-do gentleman farmer's family
before a break occurs to reveal that it is taking place in Mary's
consciousness. Travis has arrived to urge her to leave; and she, eager
to play out her story, angrily sends him away. Sensing that the
letters she has put aside are contributing to her unsettled state, he
carries them off. Mary, however, has sufficient material to sustain
her visionary dream and resumes it until the jarring repercussions
of an exploding bomb once more brings a halt.

By now, Mary has had the experience which will sustain her; and,
when Travis returns, she is ready to leave with him. She now
explains what has been troubling her: "We only know inconve-
nience now, not sorrow." And, telling him of her dream, she adds,
"I cannot forget the climate of those hours. Or life at that pitch,

eventful—not happy, no, but strung like a harp." But she bemoans the fact that he removed the letters so that she has been "left with a fragment torn out of a day. . . ." As it so happens, Travis has been reading the letters and is therefore able to provide the information which completes Mary's knowledge.

The past narrative of the letters centers upon the theme of mutability and presents three variations of it: the natural change of the seasons, the threat of emotional dislocation which accompanies growing up, and the sudden thrust of accidental death. The change of seasons provides the immediate occasion for the action. It is the day before a new school term; and, since two sons of the family, Robert and Lucius, are to depart before the day is out, the family is having a farewell walk across the fields which compose "the estate the brothers [will] not see again for so long." Sarah, the second eldest sister and the character whose being Mary inhabits, is walking with her younger sister Henrietta. The girls have been the most intimate and congenial of friends, and their relationship is the emotional center of the story; on this day Sarah first realizes that she is in love with Eugene, the friend of her eldest brother Fitzgeorge, and that her present liaison with Henrietta must inevitably alter. As she and Henrietta walk, Fitzgeorge and Eugene ride up, and the latter dismounts to walk beside Sarah.

Later, when the family has gathered in the parlor, Eugene included, Henrietta makes it evident to Sarah that she understands what has happened and what is happening. She is the stronger of the two sisters, and, "It had always been she who with one fierce act destroyed any toy that might be outgrown." This statement carries an ominous note of foreshadowing, but this fact does not become apparent until Travis takes over from Mary to complete the story. He tells of a letter written to Robert by Fitzgeorge in his old age recalling the time a friend (who in the context must be Eugene) who was killed one evening in a fall from his horse while riding away from a visit. In the letter, Fitzgeorge says he has always wondered "what made the horse shy in those empty fields." Earlier in the narrative, much is made of the white handkerchief Henrietta waves in the fields when she and Sarah first sight Fitzgeorge and Eugene riding toward them. This incident, in conjunction with the hints of Henrietta's impulsive and decisive nature, suffice to suggest what or who distracted Eugene's horse. The drama of the family letters, or more precisely Henrietta's perverse motivation and Sarah's evident tragedy, prove salutary for Mary. She takes evident satisfaction in being able to tell Travis, "I have had a sister called Henrietta."

Though the relationship between Mary and her dream and its significance have been stressed, the rich evocation of the earlier time and the delicate rendering of the emotional undercurrent between Sarah and her sister give this story its engaging intensity. This ability to project in a brief compass the flesh and anatomy of a completely realized world makes Elizabeth Bowen a superior short-story writer. This ability reaches its zenith in "The Happy Autumn Fields," "The Disinherited," "Her Table Spread," "Summer Night," and "Ivy Gripped the Steps." While Miss Bowen has been well treated by short-story anthologists in recent years, it is regrettable that each of these works, excepting "Her Table Spread," is of a length which editors must generally forego.

CHAPTER 6

The Bowen Critics

I *Pro and Con*

When William Heath published his *Elizabeth Bowen: An Introduction to Her Novels* in 1961, the only book-length study of her
work before this one, he pointed out how unfortunate she had been
in her critics: "her achievement has been least understood by those
who have admired it most extravagantly."[1] Her admirers, who had
seen her as tastefully feministic, had missed, in Heath's words,
"the toughness inherent in her intellect and essential to her art."[2]
Although the volume of Bowen criticism in the intervening years
has been modest, the quality of criticism has been responsible in a
way that the commentary Heath surveyed was not. Those critics
most impressed with her have supported their position with
thoughtful textual studies. Those who have carried a case against
her have been less impressive because they have not always demonstrated their generalizations in a convincing manner.

The adverse critics have been most troubled by Miss Bowen's
outlook, which they see as too narrow and as overly concerned with
marginal aspects of life; they are also troubled too by her artistry
which they believe has been content to rework the same materials
and which projects a sense of reality that is uncomfortably filmy
rather than substantially firm. John McCormick, for example, in
*Catastrophe and Imagination: An Interpretation of the Recent
English and American Novel* (1957), argues that Miss Bowen (along
with several of her British contemporaries) "consigned themselves
to the limbo of the minor by their preoccupation with manners,
their nostalgic theme of the bright past against the grey present.
One is tempted to say that without idea the novel of manners tends
to a feminine preoccupation with technique, the proliferation of
detail that is fascinating in itself but ultimately distracting, as in
the later novels of Elizabeth Bowen. . . ."[3]

In *The Contemporary English Novel*, Frederick Karl devotes a full chapter to Miss Bowen in which, while finding much in her work to admire, he pursues a fundamental line of devaluation at greater length than has anyone else. For Karl, the Bowen novelistic world is too restricted: "the discerning reader is struck by her limitation of range, the fluttery concern with a miniature world, the exclusion of much that makes life exciting and significant, the complacency with which the novelist repeats both characters and themes,"[4] But much the most detailed and convincing investigation aimed at showing the limitations of Miss Bowen's style has been conducted by Geoffrey Wagner in "Elizabeth Bowen and the Artificial Novel." However, Wagner deals with only one novel, *A World of Love,* which is admittedly one of her least satisfactory efforts. Certainly, it is not difficult to agree with him that "the style has forced the story into pastiche, and thus robbed the social setting of this clever pastoral of any real universality."[5]

The critics who have most persuasively made a case for the consideration of Elizabeth Bowen as a serious novelist are Heath and, more recently, James Hall. As already suggested, Heath was the first to recognize the misleading and inhibiting nature of the criticism which sought to define Miss Bowen's work. But, while he performed the necessary service of disarming the romantic-precious approach, he most importantly disclosed through his probing analyses of the novels both their rich artistic complexities and the sturdy outlook on which they rest. Now no serious critic can write about Miss Bowen without confronting Heath and his final position: "As all of my comments have been intended to suggest, Elizabeth Bowen's fiction at its best is conscious, intelligent, even austere."[6]

The most incisive criticism since Heath is found in Hall's *The Lunatic Giant in the Living Room: The British and American Novel since 1930* (1968). Hall, who obviously gained inspiration for his title from Miss Bowen, begins his discussion of seven contemporary novelists with his chapter on Elizabeth Bowen; and he accords her new significance by insisting that she is a pioneer in establishing the stance which typifies fiction of the last few decades. Hall writes that "The new novelist thus wants deep feelings to coalesce with style, drama, participation, and, unlike Waugh, will not settle for being half-ashamed of the effort. Ideally, the once revolutionary attitudes would become absorbed experience, enliveners of continuity rather than curious discoveries, domesticated carriers of vigorous hopes. But this intense wish for depth, liveliness, and safety

meets within Miss Bowen a clarity about all the obstacles to its fulfillment—and the conflict makes her a novelist."[7]

Miss Bowen determined from the start of her career to engage the
atmosphere of her times without discounting its heaviness, but she
was determined to live meaningfully with it. Miss Bowen acquired
considerable historical significance in Hall's estimate by asking
the question, "is sensibility practical?" and in working out satis-
factorily possible answers.[8]

Numbers of recent articles about Miss Bowen in critical journals
have not entered into the general discussion of the worth or future
prospects of the author. Tacitly assuming her work worthy of consideration, they pursue their explicatory way.

II *Conclusion*

What becomes increasingly apparent about Bowen criticism is
its unanimity, or near unanimity, of agreement as it concerns her
best work. Heath and Hall have properly observed that much of
Miss Bowen's fiction is of limited value and merit and is not likely
to endure; Karl and Wagner readily admit her considerable talent
and build their devaluations largely upon secondary novels. Like
most writers, Elizabeth Bowen shows to advantage when her work
is viewed selectively. What must be concluded is that her reputation
and future rest, thus far, upon two novels and upon a half dozen
short stories of a very high merit, which is no small achievement.

When she is compared with her most distinguished predecessors
of this century—Conrad, Joyce, and Lawrence—it is evident enough
she is not a novelist of the first rank. But then the same is to be said
about all of the writers who have followed them. Undeniably, the
whole question of contemporaneous literary reputations is a tenuous
affair. It is not the right moment to be confident about Miss Bowen's
position, but there are enough signs to suggest that she is a writer
considered worthy of posterity. If she is not a George Eliot, neither
is she a Marie Corelli; perhaps she is a Charlotte Brontë or an
Elizabeth Gaskell.

We may more relevantly and confidently argue Miss Bowen's
significance for the present generation of readers. As a stylist and as
a commentator, she is important. She must be counted among the
handful of contemporary rhetoricians writing in the tradition of
distinguished English letters. For her, prose is an authentic art
form; it is her personal means of ordering and enriching her world.

As such, it provides a demonstration of the still rich resources of our language and a sense of the dignified manner in which reality can be encountered. The Greeks were noble not in spite of, but because of, their created gods; and modern man can be likewise in the face of our bomb.

If those aspects of life which have most concerned Miss Bowen are narrow, they are nonetheless highly contemporaneous. The young person wondering what to do with life and how to begin it, the misunderstanding and consequent neglect and unkindness between generations, and the pressures resulting from constant change and from complexes related to the past—these are indeed topics for our times, and they are the issues upon which Elizabeth Bowen has brought to bear her artistic gifts and her exemplary civilized being.

Notes and References

References to Miss Bowen's novels are to the editions published by Jonathan Cape. All but the last three, *A World of Love*, *The Little Girls*, and *Eva Trout* are in the Collected Edition. The dates of original publication are included in the text and in the bibliography.

Chapter One

1. C. M. Bowra, *Memories, 1898-1939* (London, 1966), pp. 190-91.
2. Miss Bowen records the history of her family and its ancestral home in *Bowen's Court* (London, 1964). Like other owners of large country homes, Miss Bowen found the fiscal burden of maintaining Bowen's Court beyond her in the immediate post-World War II years. Sold to a neighboring farmer who eventually tore it down, the house, as Miss Bowen observes at the close of her book, had "a clear end. Bowen's Court never lived to be a ruin . . " (p. 459).
3. *Afterthought* (London, 1961), p. 209.
4. James Hall, *The Lunatic Giant in the Living Room* (Bloomington, 1968), p. 17.
5. Walter Allen, *Tradition and Dream* (London, 1964), pp. 191-92.
6. A. Alvarez, *The Shaping Spirit* (London, 1961), p. 141.
7. A passage from *Bowen's Court* impressively amplifies this point: "One may say that while property lasted the dangerous power-idea stayed, like a sword in its scabbard, fairly safely at rest. At least, property gave my people and people like them the means to exercise power in a direct, concrete and therefore limited way. I have shown how their natures shifted direction—or the nature of the *debordement* that occurred—when property could no longer be guaranteed. Without putting up any plea for property— unnecessary, for it is unlikely to be abolished—I submit that the power loving temperament is more dangerous when it either prefers or is forced to operate in what is mainly a void. We have everything to dread from the dispossessed. In the area of ideas we see more menacing dominations than the landlord exercised over land. The outsize will is not necessarily an evil: it is a phenomenon. It must have its outsize outlet, its big task. If the right scope is not offered it, it must seize the wrong. We should be able to harness this driving force. Not the will itself but its wastefulness is the dangerous thing. . ." (pp. 455-56).

8. Graham Greene, *The Quiet American* (New York, 1957), p. 40.

9. Robert Frost, "The Oven Bird."

Chapter Three

1. Hall, p. 49.

Chapter Four

1. Heath, p. 120.

2. This allusion may seem less fanciful when it is noted that later in the novel Dinah says "in the voice of one continuing aloud a train of thought: 'You huffed and you puffed and you blew my house down'" *The Little Girls*, p. 244.

3. Mary Ellmann, "Words, Words," *The Atlantic*, 222 (November, 1968), 126.

4. Bernard Bergonzi, "Truants," *New York Review of Books*, XI (January 2, 1969), 41.

Chapter Five

1. Edward Mitchell, "Themes in Elizabeth Bowen's Short Stories," *Critique*, VIII (1969), 41.

Chapter Six

1. Heath, p. 152.

2. *Ibid.*

3. John McCormick, *Catastrophe and Imagination: An Interpretation of the Recent English and American Novel* (London, 1957), p. 93.

4. Frederick Karl, *The Contemporary English Novel* (New York, 1962), pp. 129-30.

5. Geoffrey Wagner, "Elizabeth Bowen and the Artificial Novel," *Essays in Criticism*, XIII (1963), 163.

6. Heath, p. 158.

7. Hall, p. 18.

8. *Ibid.*, p. 19.

Selected Bibliography

PRIMARY SOURCES

I. *Novels and Stories (in order of publication)*

Encounters. London: Sidgwick and Jackson, 1923.
   Fourteen short stories (republished, along with *Ann Lee's,* in *Early Stories,* New York: Alfred A. Knopf, 1950): "Breakfast," "Daffodils," "The Return," "The Confidante," "Requiescat," "All Saints," "The New House," "Lunch," "The Lover," "Mrs. Windermere," "The Shadowy Third," "The Evil That Men Do—," "Sunday Evening," "Coming Home."

Ann Lee's and Other Stories. London: Sidgwick and Jackson, 1926. Eleven short stories (republished, along with *Encounters,* in *Early Stories,* New York: Alfred A. Knopf, 1950): "Ann Lee's," "The Parrot," "The Visitor," "The Contessina," "Human Habitation," "The Secession," "Making Arrangements," "The Storm," "Charity," "The Back Drawing-Room," "Recent Photograph."

The Hotel. London: Constable, 1927. Republished in Cape Collected Edition, 1950.

Joining Charles. London: Constable, 1929. Republished in Cape Collected Edition, 1952. Eleven short stories: "Joining Charles," "The Jungle," "Shoes: An International Episode," "The Dancing-Mistress," "Aunt Tatty," "Dead Mabelle," "The Working Party," "Foothold," "The Cassowary," "Telling," "Mrs. Moysey."

The Last September. London: Constable, 1929. Republished in Cape Collected Edition, 1948.

Friends and Relations. London: Constable, 1931. Republished in Cape Collected Edition, 1951.

To the North. London: Victor Gollancz, 1932. Republished in Cape Collected Edition, 1952.

The Cat Jumps. London: Victor Gollancz, 1934. Republished in Cape Collected Edition, 1949. Twelve short stories: "The Tommy Crans," "The Good Girls," "The Cat Jumps," "The Last Night in the Old Home," "The Disinherited," "Maria," "Her Table Spread," "The Little Girl's Room," "Firelight in the Flat," "The Man of the Family," "The Needlecase," "The Apple-Tree."

The House in Paris. London: Victor Gollancz, 1935. Republished in Cape Collected Edition, 1949.

The Death of the Heart. London: Victor Gollancz, 1938. Republished in
Cape Collected Edition, 1948.

Look at All Those Roses. London: Victor Gollancz, 1941. Republished in
Cape Collected Edition, 1951. Fourteen short stories: "Reduced,"
"Tears, Idle Tears," "A Walk in the Woods," "A Love Story," "Look
at All Those Roses," "Attractive Modern Homes," "The Easter Egg
Party," "Love," "No. 16," "A Queer Heart," "The Girl with the Stoop,"
"Unwelcome Idea," "Oh, Madam . . . ," "Summer Night."

The Demon Lover. London: Jonathan Cape, 1945.
Published as *Ivy Gripped the Steps* in New York: Alfred A. Knopf,
1946. Republished in Cape Collected Edition, 1952. Twelve short stories: "In the Square," "Sunday Afternoon," "The Inherited Clock,"
"The Cherry Soul," "Songs My Father Sang Me," "The Demon
Lover," "Careless Talk," "The Happy Autumn Fields," "Ivy Gripped
the Steps," "Pink May," "Green Holly," "Mysterious Kor."

The Heat of the Day. London: Jonathan Cape, 1949. Republished in Cape
Collected Edition, 1954.

A World of Love. London: Jonathan Cape, 1955.

Stories by Elizabeth Bowen. New York: Alfred A. Knopf, 1959. The author's
personal selection of eighteen stories, with a preface: "Coming Home,"
"The Storm," "The Tommy Crans," "Her Table Spread," "The Dis-
inherited," "The Easter Egg Party," "No. 16," "Reduced," "Look at
All Those Roses," "A Love Story," "Summer Night," "Songs My Father
Sang Me," "The Inherited Clock," "Sunday Afternoon," "The Demon
Lover," "Ivy Gripped the Steps," "The Happy Autumn Fields," "My-
sterious Kor."

The Little Girls. London: Jonathan Cape, 1964.

A Day in the Dark and Other Stories. London: Jonathan Cape, 1965. Twenty
short stories: "A Day in the Dark," "The Disinherited," "Breakfast,"
"Reduced," "Her Table Spread," "I Hear You Say So," "Summer
Night," "Gone Away," "Mysterious Kor," "A Love Story," "The
Dancing-Mistress," "Look at All Those Roses," "Hand in Glove,"
"The Demon Lover," "No. 16," "The Cheery Soul," "The Happy
Autumn Fields," "The Dolt's Tale," "The Cat Jumps," "Ivy Gripped
the Steps."

Eva Trout. London, Jonathan Cape, 1969.

II. *Books of Nonfiction (in order of publication)*

Bowen's Court. London: Longmans, Green and Co., 1942. History of the
Bowen family and its home.

Seven Winters. London: Longmans, Green and Co., 1942. Brief auto-
biography.

English Novelists. Longon: Collins, 1946. Short literary history.

Collected Impressions. London: Longmans, Green and Co., 1950. Consists of essays, prefaces, and reviews.

The Shelbourne: A Center of Dublin Life for More Than a Century. London: George G. Harrap and Co., 1951. Social history.

A Time in Rome. New York: Alfred A. Knopf, 1960. Recounts seven months spent in Rome.

Afterthought. Pieces about Writing. London: Longmans, Green and Co., 1962. Comprises broadcasts, prefaces, reflective sketches, reviews, and travel pieces.

III. *Play*

Castle Anna. A play, coauthored by John Perry. Unpublished. First performed in London in March, 1948.

SECONDARY SOURCES

ALLEN, WALTER. *Tradition and Dream: A Critical Survey of British and American Fiction from the 1920s to the Present Day.* London: Phoenix House, 1964. Comments are necessarily brief but are pointedly astute.

BROOKE, JOCELYN. *Elizabeth Bowen.* London: Longmans, Green and Co. for the British Council and the National Book League, 1952. Though not without some critical insights, this brief survey is chiefly an appreciation.

COLLINS, A. S. *English Literature in the Twentieth Century.* London: University Tutorial Press, 1962. Best brief survey of the early novels.

DAICHES, DAVID. "The Novels of Elizabeth Bowen," *English Journal*, XXXVIII (1949), 305-13. Reasonable if limited general consideration.

DORENKAMP, ANGELA G. " 'Fall or Leap': Bowen's *The Heat of the Day*," *Critique*, 10 (1968), 13-21. Examines tensions centered in imagery and language.

FRASER, G. S. *The Modern Writer and His World.* London: Derek Verschoyle, 1953. Performs a useful task of placing Elizabeth Bowen among her contemporaries.

GREENE, GEORGE. "Elizabeth Bowen: Imagination as Therapy," *Perspective*, XIV (1965), 42-52. Cordial discussion of the four novels preceding *Eva Trout.* Insights into *The Little Girls* are especially illuminating.

HALL, JAMES. *The Lunatic Giant in the Drawing Room: The British and American Novel since 1930.* Bloomington: Indiana University Press, 1968. The chapter on Elizabeth Bowen, "The Giant Located: Elizabeth Bowen," is composed chiefly of the best analysis of *The Death of the Heart.*

HARDWICK, ELIZABETH, "Elizabeth Bowen's Fiction," *Partisan Review*, XVI (1949), 114-21. One of the few thoughtful attacks made against Miss Bowen's reputation.

HARKNESS, BRUCE. "The Fiction of Elizabeth Bowen," *English Journal*, XLIV (1955), 499-506. Too much is covered too briefly to be more than suggestive.

HEATH, WILLIAM. *Elizabeth Bowen: An Introduction to Her Novels.* Madison: The University of Wisconsin Press, 1961. The only previous book-length study, it is a provocative, sophisticated study which belies the word "Introduction" in the title.

HEINEMANN, ALISON. "The Indoor Landscape in Bowen's *The Death of the Heart*," *Critique*, 10 (1968), 5-12. Considers the emotional importance of objects in the novel.

KARL, FREDERICK. *The Contemporary English Novel.* New York: Farrar, Straus and Cudahy, 1962. Includes a chapter entitled, "The World of Elizabeth Bowen," which discusses several novels in a reasonable if somewhat adverse manner.

McCORMICK, JOHN. *Catastrophe and Imagination: An Interpretation of the Recent English and American Novel.* London: Longmans, Green and Co., 1957. Several passing, hostile references to Elizabeth Bowen's work.

MITCHELL, EDWARD. "Themes in Elizabeth Bowen's Short Stories," *Critique*, VIII (1966), 41-54. Valuable as the first effort to organize Miss Bowen's stories; identifies four basic thematic patterns.

O'FAOLAIN, SEAN. *The Vanishing Hero: Studies in Novelists of the Twenties.* London: Eyre and Spottiswood, 1956. Though only the earliest of Miss Bowen's novels qualify for the author's subject, the chapter on her work, "Romance does not pay," is intelligent and praiseworthy.

RUPP, RICHARD HENRY. "The Post-War Fiction of Elizabeth Bowen," *Xavier University Studies*, IV (1965), 55-67. Sees the later work as a falling away from *The Death of the Heart* and seeks to account for this.

SAUL, GEORGE BRANDON. "The Short Stories of Elizabeth Bowen," *Arizona Quarterly*, XXI (1965), 53-59. General introductory investigation of the story collections approached chronologically. Saul supports the contention that Miss Bowen's success in the genre is intermittent rather than developmental.

SEWARD, BARBARA. "Elizabeth Bowen's World of Impoverished Love," *College English*, XVIII (1956), 30-37. Heavily rides betrayal of innocence theme.

SHARP, SISTER M. CORONA, O. S. U. "The House as Setting and Symbol in Three Novels by Elizabeth Bowen," *Xavier University Studies*, II (1963), 93-103. The three novels are *The Last September*, *The House in Paris*, and *The Death of the Heart*.

VAN DUYN, MONA. "Pattern and Pilgrimage: A Reading of *The Death of the Heart*," *Critique*, IV (1961), 52-66. Rich complexity and subtle control of this novel are tellingly illuminated.

WAGNER, GEOFFREY. "Elizabeth Bowen and the Artificial Novel," *Essays in Criticism*, XIII (1963), 155-63. Perhaps the most intelligent anti-Bowen article written, but limited by concern with a single novel, *The World of Love*.

Index

(In the alphabetical listing of stories, novels, and collections, titles are listed without regard to the beginning articles "A" and "The.")